THE NEW YELLOW BOOK: GOVERNMENT AUDITING STANDARDS, 2018 VERSION

BY REBECCA A. MEYER, CPA, CGMA

T0338240

Notice to readers

The New Yellow Book: Government Auditing Standards, 2018 Version is intended solely for use in continuing professional education and not as a reference. It does not represent an official position of the Association of International Certified Professional Accountants, and it is distributed with the understanding that the author and publisher are not rendering legal, accounting, or other professional services in the publication. This course is intended to be an overview of the topics discussed within, and the author has made every attempt to verify the completeness and accuracy of the information herein. However, neither the author nor publisher can guarantee the applicability of the information found herein. If legal advice or other expert assistance is required, the services of a competent professional should be sought.

Special note: COVID-19 resources

The Association, the global voice of the American Institute of CPAs and the Chartered Institute of Management Accountants, is taking the Coronavirus (COVID-19) very seriously.

We are continually monitoring the virus' impact on our members and the profession. For the most up-to-date information on this topic, please visit the AICPA's Coronavirus Resource Center at www.aicpa.org/news/aicpa-coronavirus-resource-center.html.

For topic-specific updates, please visit the following resource centers.

COVID-19 Resource Center	Website
Audit and accounting	www.aicpa.org/interestareas/frc/covid19.html
Forensic and valuation services	www.aicpa.org/interestareas/forensicandvaluation/covid-19.html
Management accounting	www.aicpa.org/interestareas/businessindustryandgovernment/management-accounting-covid-19.html
Personal financial planning	www.aicpa.org/interestareas/personalfinancialplanning/covid19.html
Small firm	www.aicpa.org/membership/small-firms.html
Tax	www.aicpa.org/interestareas/tax/covid19.html

ISBN 978-1-11978-463-0 (Paper)
ISBN 978-1-11978-471-5 (ePDF)
ISBN 978-1-11978-470-8 (ePub)
ISBN 978-1-11978-472-2 (oBook)

Course Code: **746631**
YBRV GS-0420-0C
Revised: **May 2020**

SKY10021800_102120

Table of Contents

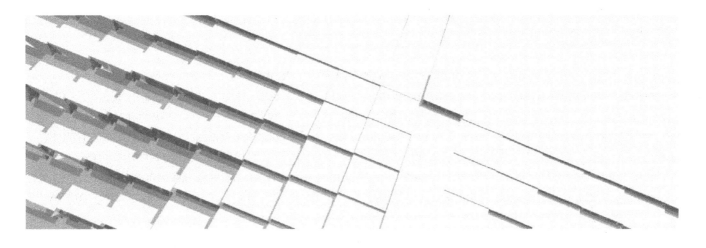

Foundation and Principles for the Use and Application of *Government Auditing Standards*

Learning objectives

- Recognize why engagements are conducted in accordance with generally accepted government auditing standards (GAGAS or Yellow Book).

- Recall revisions brought about by the 2018 revision to GAGAS.

- Identify the types of engagements that may be conducted under GAGAS.

What is GAGAS?

Generally accepted government auditing standards (GAGAS), issued by the U.S. Government Accountability Office (GAO), provide a framework of audit and attest standards for use by auditors of government entities, functions, activities, and programs, as well as for government assistance administered by nonfederal entities. GAGAS provides the foundation for auditors to lead by example in areas of independence, transparency, accountability, and quality through the audit process. The standards provide a framework for performing high-quality audit work with competence, integrity, objectivity, and independence with the overall objective of providing accountability and helping improve government operations and services.

Known widely as the "Yellow Book," GAGAS aids the auditing process in four ways.

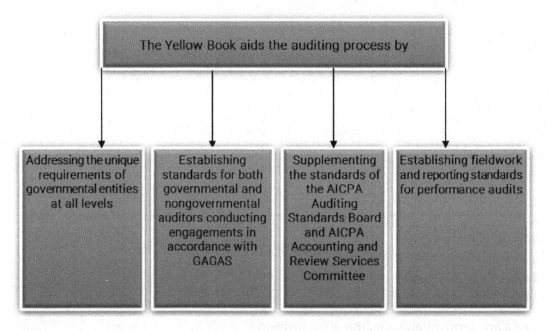

The Yellow Book aids the auditing process by

| Addressing the unique requirements of governmental entities at all levels | Establishing standards for both governmental and nongovernmental auditors conducting engagements in accordance with GAGAS | Supplementing the standards of the AICPA Auditing Standards Board and AICPA Accounting and Review Services Committee | Establishing fieldwork and reporting standards for performance audits |

In this course, the terms GAS, GAGAS, and Yellow Book are used interchangeably.

Brief history of *Government Auditing Standards*

Beginning in the mid-1960s, both the number and the dollar amount of federal government programs and services increased substantially. This increase brought with it a demand for full accountability from those entrusted with public funds and the responsibility for managing government programs and services properly.

Origin of the standards

In 1969, the Comptroller General of the United States held a series of meetings with a group of state auditors and federal officials. These meetings identified a need to improve government auditing. One of the areas identified was the absence of formal GAS. In July 1969, the GAO initiated plans for an audit standards work group charged with the objective of developing GAS.

In 1970, the audit standards work group started the survey and research work on which the original 1972 standards were based. The work group included representatives from the GAO, federal departments and agencies, state and local government auditors, and professional organizations including the AICPA. Assistance was also provided by academics and public interest groups. In June 1972, the Comptroller General issued the original version of the Yellow Book, *Standards for Audits of Governmental Organizations, Programs, Activities & Functions*.

Yellow Book revisions

In 1979, the GAO started a project to revise the standards. Based on comments and suggestions the GAO had received since the standards were originally issued, a draft of proposed revised standards was prepared and released for comment in August 1980. Comments received were analyzed and evaluated for appropriate consideration in arriving at the final draft standards. The 1981 revision of GAGAS was signed by the Comptroller General on February 27, 1981.

In November 1985, the GAO started a project to clarify, update, and revise the 1981 revision of the Yellow Book. In December 1985, the Comptroller General appointed an Auditing Standards Advisory Council (ASAC) to advise him and the GAO on revising the standards. The council was composed of individuals from federal, state, and local governments; public accounting; academia; and other special interest groups. On March 16, 1987, an exposure draft was released for comment and was sent to audit officials at all levels of government and members of the public accounting profession, academia, professional organizations, and public interest groups. Comments received were analyzed and evaluated, and appropriate changes were made in the final draft. The final revised standards were released in August 1988, superseding the 1981 revision.

In July 1993, an exposure draft was released proposing changes to the 1988 Yellow Book revision. A revision, *Government Auditing Standards: 1994 Revision*, was released on June 6, 1994. Its provisions were effective for financial audits of periods ending on or after January 1, 1995, and performance audits beginning on or after January 1, 1995.

After the issuance of the 1994 revision of the Yellow Book, three amendments were issued as follows:

- Amendment No. 1: *Documentation Requirements When Assessing Control Risk at Maximum for Controls Significantly Dependent Upon Computerized Information Systems*, issued May 1999
- Amendment No. 2: *Auditor Communication*, issued July 1999
- Amendment No. 3: *Independence*, issued January 2002

In June 2003, the GAO released an omnibus revision to the Yellow Book. The standards became applicable for financial audits and attestation engagements of periods ending on or after January 1, 2004, and for performance audits beginning on or after January 1, 2004.

In July 2007, the GAO issued an omnibus revision to the Yellow Book. The 2007 Yellow Book became applicable for financial audits and attestation engagements for periods beginning on or after January 1, 2008, and for performance audits beginning on or after January 1, 2008.

In December 2011, the GAO issued *Government Auditing Standards (2011 Revision)*, which superseded the 2007 revision.

In April 2017, GAO issued an exposure draft containing proposed changes to *Government Auditing Standards, December 2011 Revision.* The final document, entitled *Government Auditing Standards: 2018 Revision*, was issued on July 17, 2018. It is effective for financial audits, attestation engagements, and reviews of financial statements for periods ending on or after June 30, 2020 and was effective for performance audits performed as of July 1, 2019. The independence provisions of the *2018 revision* are effective as of July 1, 2019 for fiscal year engagements ending on June 30, 2020. The revision supersedes the December 2011 revision of the standards, the 2005 *Government Auditing Standards: Guidance on GAGAS Requirements for Continuing Professional Education*, and the 2014 *Government Auditing Standards: Guidance for Understanding the New Peer Review Ratings.*

This course presents the requirements and guidance found in GAGAS based on *Government Auditing Standards*: 2018 Revision.

The 2018 Yellow Book

The 2018 Yellow Book contains significant changes from the 2011 Yellow Book that are aimed at reinforcing the principles of transparency and accountability and strengthening the framework for high-quality governmental audit and attest engagements. These changes are summarized into the following categories:

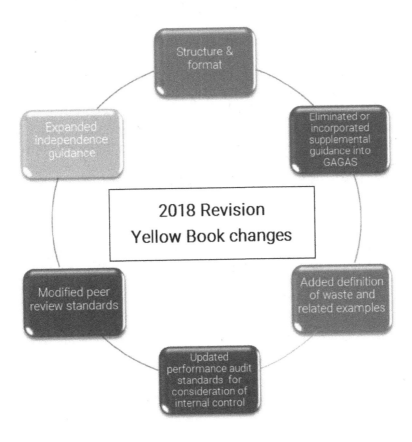

Clarity in the new GAGAS format

The format of all chapters has been revised to differentiate GAGAS requirements from application guidance related to those requirements.

GAGAS requirements in the 2018 revision are differentiated from application guidance by borders surrounding the text. The requirements are followed immediately by application guidance that relates directly to the preceding requirements.

Supplemental guidance previously included in the appendix of the 2011 revision has been either incorporated into the individual chapters or removed. Additionally, content previously found in *Government Auditing Standards: Guidance on GAGAS Requirements for Continuing Professional Education* (GAO-05-568G, April 2005) and *Government Auditing Standards: Guidance for Understanding the New Peer Review Ratings* (D06602, January 2014) has either been incorporated into the 2018 revision or removed as guidance. These two publications will be retired upon the effective date of the 2018 revision.

In the 2018 revision, chapters were reorganized and realigned in the following ways:

- There are nine chapters, up from seven chapters in the 2011 revision.
- Ethical principles were moved from chapter 1 to chapter 3.
- Much of the material from chapter 2 of the 2011 revision is now in chapter 1.
- The topics of independence, competence, and quality control that were previously included in chapter 3 have each been expanded and afforded their own chapters.
- Standards for financial audits have been expanded and moved to chapter 6.
- Standards for attestation engagements and reviews of financial statements have been expanded and moved to chapter 7.
- Fieldwork and reporting standards for performance audits have been expanded and moved to chapters 8 and 9.

> *Government Auditing Standards*, 2018 Revision is effective for financial audits, attestation engagements, and reviews of financial statements for periods ending on or after June 30, 2020, and for performance audits beginning on or after July 1, 2019. Early implementation is not permitted.

Acquiring the *Government Auditing Standards* publication

Obtaining a copy of the GAO *Government Auditing Standards (2018 Revision)* is highly recommended for participants of this course. A PDF version can be downloaded from www.gao.gov/yellowbook/overview.

For technical assistance regarding the Yellow Book, please call (202) 512-9535 or email yellowbook@gao.gov.

Why is GAGAS important?

Our nation's governing processes count on the concept of accountability for use of public resources and government authority. It is the responsibility of management and officials entrusted with public resources to carry out public duties and provide services to the public in an effective, efficient, economical, and ethical manner within the context of the statutory boundaries of the specific government program.

Officials and management of government programs are responsible for providing reliable, useful, and timely information for transparency and accountability of these programs and their operations as reflected in applicable laws, regulations, agreements, and standards. Legislators, oversight bodies, those charged with governance, and the public need to know whether

- management and officials manage government resources and use their authority properly and in compliance with laws and regulations;
- government programs are achieving their objectives and desired outcomes; and
- government services are provided effectively, efficiently, economically, and ethically.

In the context of GAGAS, *those charged with governance* refers to the persons responsible for supervising the strategic direction of an entity and obligations related to the accountability of an entity. This supervision includes overseeing the financial reporting process, subject matter, or program under audit, including related internal controls. Those charged with governance may also be part of the entity's management. In some audited entities, multiple parties may be charged with governance, including oversight bodies, members or staff of legislative committees, boards of directors, audit committees, or parties contracting for the engagement.

> Government audit and attest engagements are essential in providing accountability to legislators, oversight bodies, those charged with governance, and the public. GAGAS engagements provide an independent, objective, nonpartisan assessment of the stewardship, performance, or cost of government policies, programs, or operations, depending upon the type and scope of the engagement.

How does GAGAS achieve its objective?

GAGAS contains requirements and guidance dealing with ethics, independence, auditors' professional judgment and competence, quality control, peer review, conducting the engagement, and reporting.

Engagements conducted in accordance with GAGAS deliver information used for

- oversight,
- accountability,
- transparency, and
- improvements of government programs and operations.

GAGAS helps auditors in objectively obtaining and evaluating sufficient, appropriate evidence and reporting the results by providing auditing requirements and guidance. The work of auditors can lead to enhanced government management, better decision making and oversight, effective and efficient operations, and accountability and transparency for resources and results when they comply with GAGAS in the performance of their work and in reporting the results.

Who has to follow GAGAS?

An auditor has a responsibility to comply with professional standards and the applicable legal and regulatory requirements in any audit or attest engagement that they accept. As part of this responsibility, an auditor needs to determine whether the entity is subject to *Government Auditing Standards*.

Not all engagements are required to be conducted in accordance with GAGAS. Auditors should review whether laws, regulations, contracts, grant agreements, and policies to which the entity is subject contain provisions that would require that engagements be conducted in accordance with GAGAS. In addition, many auditors and audit organizations voluntarily choose to conduct their work in accordance with GAGAS. Auditors must follow the requirements and guidance in GAGAS in totality for engagements pertaining to government entities, programs, activities, and functions, and to government assistance administered by contractors, not-for-profit entities, and other nongovernmental entities when the use of GAGAS is required or voluntarily adopted.

The laws, regulations, and other authoritative sources that require the use of GAGAS include:

- The Inspector General Act of 1978, as amended (5 USC App.), requires that the federal inspectors general appointed under that act comply with GAGAS for audits of federal establishments, organizations, programs, activities, and functions.
- The Chief Financial Officers Act of 1990 (Public Law 101-576), as expanded by the Government Management Reform Act of 1994 (Public Law 103-356), requires that GAGAS be followed in audits of major executive branch departments' and agencies' financial statements. The Accountability of Tax Dollars Act of 2002 (Public Law 107-289) generally extends this requirement to most executive agencies not subject to the Chief Financial Officers Act.
- The Single Audit Act Amendments of 1996 (Public Law 104-156) requires that GAGAS be followed in audits of state and local governments and not-for-profit entities that receive federal awards. Title 2 U.S. Code of Federal Regulations Part 200, *Uniform Administrative Requirements, Cost Principles, and Audit Requirements for Federal Awards* (Uniform Guidance) — which provides the government-wide guidelines and policies on conducting compliance audits to comply with the Single Audit Act — reiterates the requirement to use GAGAS in a single audit.

Examples of engagements requiring the use of GAGAS are when a nonfederal entity receives

- grant funds from a federal agency (such as Department of Health and Human Services);
- federal funds from a passthrough entity; or
- federal funds from a state or local government agency.

Other laws, regulations, or authoritative sources may mandate the use of GAGAS. For instance, state and local laws and regulations may obligate auditors at the state and local government levels to follow

GAGAS. Moreover, the terms of an agreement or contract or federal audit guidelines pertaining to program requirements may mandate a requirement to follow GAGAS. Being aware of such other laws, regulations, or authoritative sources may assist auditors in conducting their work in accordance with the required standards.

Even if not required to do so, auditors, both in the United States and in other countries, voluntarily follow GAGAS as they find it useful in conducting engagements pertaining to federal, state, and local government programs as well as engagements pertaining to state and local government awards that contractors, not-for-profit entities, and other nongovernmental entities administer.

Types of GAGAS users

A wide range of auditors and audit organizations follow GAGAS in their audits of government entities, entities that receive government awards, and other entities. These auditors and audit organizations may also be subject to additional requirements unique to their environments. Examples of the various types of users who may be required or may elect to use GAGAS include the following:

Contract auditors

Audit organizations that specialize in conducting engagements pertaining to government acquisitions and contract administration

CPA firms

Public accounting organizations in the private sector that provide audit, attestation, or review services under contract to government entities or recipients of government funds

Federal inspectors general

Government audit organizations within federal agencies that conduct engagements and investigations relating to the programs and operations of their agencies and issue reports both to agency management and to third parties external to the audited entity

Federal agency internal auditors

Internal government audit organizations associated with federal agencies that conduct engagements and investigations relating to the programs and operations of their agencies

Municipal auditors

Elected or appointed officials in government audit organizations in the United States at the city, county, and other local government levels

State auditors

Elected or appointed officials in audit organizations in the governments of the 50 states, the District of Columbia , and U.S. territories

Supreme audit institutions

National government audit organizations, in the United States or elsewhere, typically headed by a comptroller general or auditor general

Types of GAGAS engagements

There are several types of engagements that audit organizations may conduct in accordance with GAGAS. GAGAS specifies that the guidance provided is not intended to limit or require the types of engagements that may be conducted in accordance with GAGAS.

> All GAGAS engagements begin with objectives, and those objectives determine the type of engagement to be conducted and the applicable standards to be followed. GAGAS classifies financial audits, attestation engagements, reviews of financial statements, and performance audits, as defined by their objectives, as the types of engagements that are covered by GAGAS.

In some GAGAS engagements, the standards applicable to the specific objective will be obvious. For instance, if the objective is to express an opinion on financial statements, the standards for financial audits apply. However, some engagements may have objectives that could be met using more than one approach. This may occur, for example, if the objective is to determine the reliability of performance measures. Auditors can perform this work in accordance with either the standards for attestation engagements or performance audits.

GAGAS requirements and guidance apply to the types of engagements that auditors may conduct in accordance with GAGAS as follows:

Financial audits
- The requirements and application guidance in chapters 1–6 of GAGAS apply

Attestation & reviews of financial statements
- The requirements and guidance in chapters 1–5 and 7 of GAGAS apply

Performance audits
- The requirements and guidance in chapters 1–5, 8 and 9 apply

What are financial audits?

Financial audits provide an independent assessment of whether an entity's reported financial information (such as financial condition, results, and use of resources) is presented fairly, in all material respects, in accordance with recognized criteria. Financial audits conducted in accordance with GAGAS include financial statement audits and other related financial audits.

The primary purpose of a financial statement audit is for an auditor to provide financial statement users with an opinion on whether an entity's financial statements are presented fairly, in all material respects, in accordance with an applicable financial reporting framework. Financial statement audits conducted in accordance with GAGAS include reporting on internal control over financial reporting and on compliance with provisions of laws, regulations, contracts, and grant agreements that have a material effect on the financial statements.

Other types of financial audits conducted in accordance with GAGAS entail various scopes of work, including

- obtaining sufficient, appropriate evidence to form an opinion on a single financial statement or specified elements, accounts, or line items of a financial statement;
- issuing letters (commonly referred to as comfort letters) for underwriters and certain other requesting parties;
- auditing compliance and internal control requirements relating to one or more government programs; and
- conducting an audit of internal control over financial reporting that is integrated with an audit of financial statements (integrated audit).

What are attestation engagements?

An *attestation engagement* is one in which an auditor measures or evaluates subject matter or an assertion by an outside party in accordance with criteria suitable under the circumstances. Attestation engagements can cover a broad range of financial or nonfinancial objectives about the subject matter or assertion depending on the needs of the user. The type of attestation engagement governs the level of work performed by the auditor and the level of assurance provided. The three types of attestation engagements and the level of assurance associated with each of them are as follows:

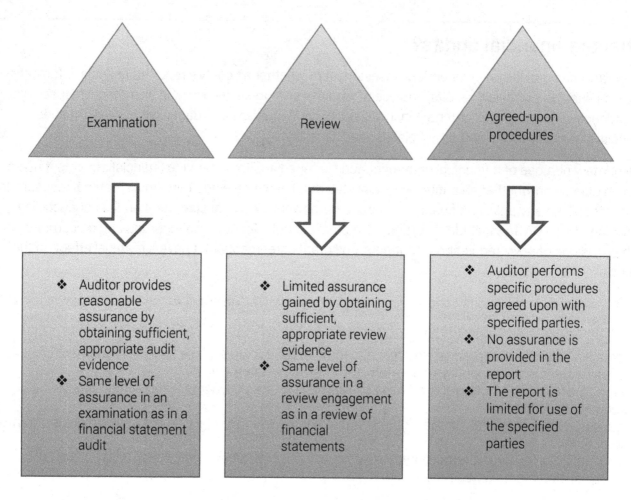

The form of the subject matter of an attestation engagement may include

- historical or prospective performance or condition, historical or prospective financial information, performance measurements, or backlog data;
- physical characteristics such as narrative descriptions or square footage of facilities;
- historical events, for instance, the price of a market basket of goods on a certain date;
- analyses such as break-even analyses;
- systems and processes such as internal control; and
- behavior such as corporate governance, compliance with laws and regulations, and human resource practices.

What are reviews of financial statements?

The objective of a *review* of financial statements is to obtain limited assurance as a basis for reporting whether the auditor is aware of any material modifications that should be made to the financial statements in order for them to be in accordance with the applicable financial reporting framework. It is less in scope than an audit and does not include, among other things, obtaining an understanding of internal control and assessing fraud risk. Reviews of financial statements under GAGAS are performed under AR-C section 90, *Review of Financial Statements* (AICPA, *Professional Standards*).

What are performance audits?

A *performance audit* provides objective analysis, findings, and conclusions. The purpose, among other things, is to help management and those charged with governance and oversight with improving program performance and operations, reducing costs, facilitating decision making by parties responsible for overseeing or initiating corrective action, and contributing to public accountability.

Different from financial audits, performance audit objectives can vary widely. Performance audit objectives include assessments of program effectiveness, economy, and efficiency; internal control; compliance; and prospective analysis. They may also relate to the current status or condition of a program. These overall objectives are not mutually exclusive, and each performance audit may have several objectives. For instance, a performance audit with an objective of determining or evaluating program effectiveness may involve an additional objective of evaluating the program's internal controls.

Knowledge check

1. An audit in accordance with the Yellow Book may be conducted because of all **except**

    a. Contractual requirements.
    b. Requirements in regulations.
    c. Voluntary choice.
    d. GAAS.

Terms used in this course and in GAGAS

The Yellow Book provides definitions of terms utilized in the standards. That guidance specifies that if terminology differs from that used at an organization subject to GAGAS, auditors are to use professional judgment to determine if there is an equivalent term. Some terms provided include:

Audit	Either a financial audit or performance audit conducted in accordance with GAGAS.
Audit organization	A government audit entity or a public accounting firm or other audit entity that conducts GAGAS engagements
Audit report	A report issued as a result of a financial audit, attestation engagement, review of financial statements, or performance audit conducted in accordance with GAGAS
Audited entity	The entity that is subject to a GAGAS engagement, whether that engagement is a financial audit, attestation engagement, review of financial statements, or performance audit
Auditor	An individual assigned to planning, directing, performing engagement procedures, or reporting on GAGAS engagements (including work on audits, attestation engagements, and reviews of financial statements) regardless of job title. Therefore, individuals who may have the title auditor, information technology auditor, analyst, practitioner, evaluator, inspector, or another similar title are considered auditors under GAGAS.
Control objective	The aim or purpose of specified controls; control objectives address the risks related to achieving an entity's objectives.
Engagement	A financial audit, attestation engagement, review of financial statements, or performance audit conducted in accordance with GAGAS
Engagement team (or audit team)	Auditors assigned to planning, directing, performing engagement procedures, or reporting on GAGAS engagements
Engaging party	The party that engages the auditor to conduct the GAGAS engagement
Entity objective	What an entity wants to achieve; entity objectives are intended to meet the entity's mission, strategic plan, and goals, as well as the requirements of applicable laws and regulations.
External audit organization	An audit organization that issues reports to third parties external to the audited entity, either exclusively or in addition to issuing reports to senior management and those charged with governance of the audited entity
Internal audit organization	An audit organization that is accountable to senior management and those charged with governance of the audited entity and that does not generally issue reports to third parties external to the audited entity
Responsible party	The party responsible for a GAGAS engagement's subject matter
Specialist	An individual or organization possessing special skill or knowledge in a particular field other than accounting or auditing that assists auditors in conducting engagements. A specialist may be either an internal specialist or an external specialist.

Knowledge check

2. All of the following meet the definition of an "auditor" within the guidance of GAGAS **except**:

    a. An actuary engaged by an audit team to assist in the performance of an engagement subject to GAGAS.

    b. An engagement partner responsible for planning a performance audit conducted in accordance with GAGAS.

    c. A federal internal inspector who reports on investigations related to the programs and operations of the federal agency.

    d. A staff person performing agreed-upon procedures over a contract that is required to be conducted in accordance with the Yellow Book.

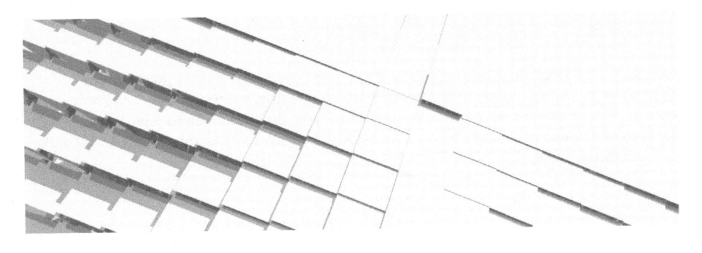

Chapter 2

General Requirements for Complying with *Government Auditing Standards*

Learning objectives

- Identify the two categories of professional requirements used in generally accepted government auditing standards (GAGAS or the Yellow Book).

- Recognize the relationship between GAGAS and other professional standards.

Introduction

Chapter 2 of the Yellow Book includes general requirements for complying with GAGAS that are applicable to all GAGAS engagements. The information relates to how auditors conducting GAGAS engagements identify and apply the requirements contained within GAGAS. It also contains requirements for using other audit standards in conjunction with GAGAS and for reporting compliance with GAGAS in the audit report.

Complying with GAGAS

GAGAS uses a format designed to allow auditors to quickly identify requirements and application guidance related to those requirements. GAGAS requirements are differentiated from application guidance by borders surrounding the text. The requirements are followed immediately by related explanatory material in the form of application guidance.

Paragraphs 2.02–2.06 of GAGAS	Requirements: Complying with GAGAS
	2.02 GAGAS uses two categories of requirements, identified by specific terms, to describe the degree of responsibility they impose on auditors and audit organizations:
	a. Unconditional requirements: Auditors and audit organizations must comply with an unconditional requirement in all cases where such requirement is relevant. GAGAS uses *must* to indicate an unconditional requirement.
	b. Presumptively mandatory requirements: Auditors and audit organizations must comply with a presumptively mandatory requirement in all cases where such a requirement is relevant except in rare circumstances discussed in paragraphs 2.03, 2.04, and 2.08. GAGAS uses *should* to indicate a presumptively mandatory requirement.
	2.03 In rare circumstances, auditors and audit organizations may determine it necessary to depart from a relevant presumptively mandatory requirement. In such rare circumstances, auditors should perform alternative procedures to achieve the intent of that requirement.
	2.04 If, in rare circumstances, auditors judge it necessary to depart from a relevant presumptively mandatory requirement, they must document their justification for the departure and how the alternative procedures performed in the circumstances were sufficient to achieve the intent of that requirement.
	2.05 Auditors should have an understanding of the entire text of applicable chapters of GAGAS, including application guidance, and any amendments that GAO issued, to understand the intent of the requirements and to apply the requirements properly.
	2.06 Auditors should consider applicable GAO-issued GAGAS interpretive guidance in conducting and reporting on GAGAS engagements.

Not every paragraph of GAGAS carries a requirement. As noted previously, GAGAS identifies the requirements through use of specific formatting. Introductory material is also included, which provides context relevant to a proper understanding of a GAGAS chapter or section. Understanding the entire text of applicable GAGAS includes an understanding of any financial audit, attestation, and reviews of financial statement standards incorporated by reference.

GAGAS anticipates that, occasionally, an auditor may need to depart from a relevant presumptively mandatory requirement. Therefore, some flexibility is contained within the standards. However, departure from a presumptively mandatory requirement is expected to arise only when the requirement would be ineffective in achieving the intent of the requirement. Auditors must document their reasoning for departing from the presumptively mandatory requirement, as well as the alternate procedures performed and how those procedures complied with the overall objective.

The application guidance found in GAGAS provides further explanation of the requirements and guidance for applying them. It is intended to explain more clearly what a requirement means or aims to address or include examples of procedures that may be appropriate in the circumstances. Some application guidance may provide background information on the matter being addressed. Although application guidance does not in itself impose a requirement, it is relevant to the proper application of the requirements. *May*, *might*, and *could* are used to describe these actions and procedures.

Relationship between GAGAS and other professional standards

Paragraph 2.11 of GAGAS	Requirement: Relationship between GAGAS and Other Professional Standards
	2.11 When auditors cite compliance with both GAGAS and another set of standards, such as those listed in paragraphs 2.13, 2.15, 6.01, and 7.01, auditors should refer to paragraph 2.17 for the requirements for citing compliance with GAGAS. In addition to citing GAGAS, auditors may also cite the use of other standards in their reports when they have also met the requirements for citing compliance with the other standards. Auditors should refer to the other set of standards for the basis for citing compliance with those standards.

GAGAS incorporates by reference the following professional standards of the American Institute of Certified Public Accountants (AICPA):

- Statements on Auditing Standards (SASs)
- Statements on Standards for Attestation Engagements (SSAE)
- AR-C section 90, Reviews of Financial Statements

Although not incorporated by reference, GAGAS has included the following examples of standards that auditors may elect to follow in conjunction with GAGAS:

- The International Auditing and Assurance Standards Board (IAASB) has established standards that apply to financial audits and assurance engagements. Auditors may elect to follow the IAASB standards and the related International Standards on Auditing and International Standards on Assurance Engagements in conjunction with GAGAS.
- The Public Company Accounting Oversight Board (PCAOB) has established professional standards that apply to financial audits and attestation engagements for issuers. Auditors may elect to use the PCAOB standards in conjunction with GAGAS.

In addition, although not incorporated into the standards, auditors may be required to, or choose to, follow certain guidance. For example

- For financial audits, attestation engagements, and reviews of financial statements, GAGAS does not incorporate the AICPA Code of Professional Conduct by reference, but recognizes that certain CPAs may use or may be required to use the code in conjunction with GAGAS.
- For performance audits, GAGAS does not incorporate other standards by reference, but recognizes that auditors may use or may be required to use other professional standards in conjunction with GAGAS, such as the following:
  - *International Standards for the Professional Practice of Internal Auditing*, Institute of Internal Auditors, Inc.

- *International Standards of Supreme Audit Institutions*, International Organization of Supreme Audit Institutions
- *Guiding Principles for Evaluators*, American Evaluation Association
- *The Program Evaluation Standards*, Joint Committee on Standards for Education Evaluation
- *Standards for Educational and Psychological Testing*, American Psychological Association
- *IT Standards, Guidelines, and Tools and Techniques for Audit and Assurance and Control Professionals*, Information Systems Audit and Control Association

---

Knowledge check

1. Which statement is accurate?

    a. Requirements and application guidance are differentiated by color of font.
    b. Application guidance may provide further explanation of a particular requirement.
    c. Requirements in GAGAS are what is important; application guidance provides history only.
    d. Application guidance is found in an appendix at the end of each chapter.

Stating auditor compliance with GAGAS in the audit report

GAGAS indicates how to cite compliance with GAGAS in the auditors' report.

Paragraphs 2.16–2.19 of GAGAS	Requirements: Stating Compliance with GAGAS in the Audit Report
	2.16 When auditors are required to conduct an engagement in accordance with GAGAS or are representing to others that they did so, they should cite compliance with GAGAS in the audit report as set forth in paragraphs 2.17 through 2.19.
	2.17 Auditors should include one of the following types of GAGAS compliance statements in reports on GAGAS engagements, as appropriate.
	a. Unmodified GAGAS compliance statement: Stating that the auditors conducted the engagement in accordance with GAGAS. Auditors should include an unmodified GAGAS compliance statement in the audit report when they have (1) followed unconditional and applicable presumptively mandatory GAGAS requirements or (2) followed unconditional requirements, documented justification for any departures from applicable presumptively mandatory requirements, and achieved the objectives of those requirements through other means.
	b. Modified GAGAS compliance statement: Stating either that
	i. the auditors conducted the engagement in accordance with GAGAS, except for specific applicable requirements that were not followed, or
	ii. because of the significance of the departure(s) from the requirements, the auditors were unable to and did not conduct the engagement in accordance with GAGAS.
	2.18 When auditors use a modified GAGAS statement, they should disclose in the report the applicable requirement(s) not followed, the reasons for not following the requirement(s), and how not following the requirement(s) affected or could have affected the engagement and the assurance provided.
	2.19 When auditors do not comply with applicable requirement(s), they should (1) assess the significance of the noncompliance to the engagement objectives; (2) document the assessment, along with their reasons for not following the requirement(s); and (3) determine the type of GAGAS compliance statement.

GAGAS guidance indicates that a scope limitation — such as restrictions on access to records, government officials, or other individuals needed to conduct the engagement — would be a situation where using a modified compliance statement would be applicable.

The determination of noncompliance by the auditors with applicable requirements is a matter of professional judgment, which is impacted by the significance of the requirements not followed in relation to the engagement objectives. Consideration of the individual and aggregate effect of the instances of noncompliance with GAGAS requirements is needed when determining whether an unmodified or modified GAGAS compliance statement is appropriate. Some factors that the auditor may consider regarding the type of compliance statement is as follows:

- The pervasiveness of the instance(s) of noncompliance
- The potential effect of the instance(s) of noncompliance on the sufficiency and appropriateness of evidence supporting the findings, conclusions, and recommendations
- Whether report users might misunderstand the implications of a modified or unmodified GAGAS compliance statement.

GAGAS application guidance notes that except for certain specific situations, a modified GAGAS compliance statement is used when the auditor concludes that independence of the engagement team or the audit organization is impaired because there are no safeguards effectively applied to eliminate an unacceptable threat or reduce it to an acceptable level.

Relationship of *Government Auditing Standards* to the Uniform Guidance

Audits performed under Title 2 U.S. Code of Federal Regulations Part 200, *Uniform Administrative Requirements, Cost Principles, and Audit Requirements for Federal Awards* (Uniform Guidance) require that the audit be performed in accordance with *Government Auditing Standards*. The following illustrates the three layers of requirements found in a compliance audit performed under the Uniform Guidance:

- Uniform Guidance requirements
- GAGAS requirements
- GAAS requirements

Knowledge check

2. Which of the following best describes the relationship of GAGAS and other standards?

   a. GAGAS requires the Uniform Guidance requirements to be used in the Yellow Book audit.
   b. An auditor may use GAGAS in a Uniform Guidance compliance audit but it is not required.
   c. GAAS requires the use of GAGAS in certain types of audits.
   d. GAGAS is required to be used in a Uniform Guidance compliance audit.

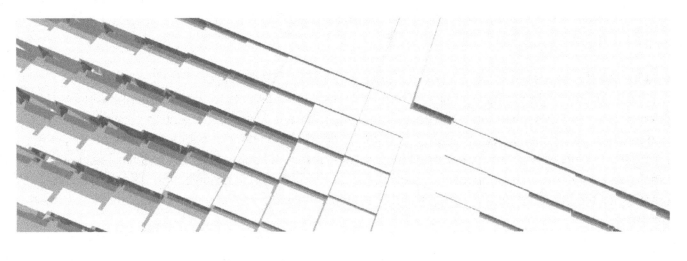

Chapter 3

Ethics, Independence, and Professional Judgment

Learning objectives

- Recognize the fundamental ethical principles for auditors in the government environment.

- Identify requirements related to independence in an engagement conducted in accordance with generally accepted government auditing standards (GAGAS).

- Recognize the GAGAS conceptual framework approach to independence.

- Identify the auditor's responsibility when providing nonaudit services to a nonfederal entity.

- Recognize the role of professional judgment in a GAGAS engagement.

Introduction

Chapter 3, *Ethics, Independence, and Professional Judgment*, of GAGAS is organized in three parts. The first section, ethical principles, contains no requirements. Instead it sets forth fundamental ethical principles for auditors operating in the government environment. The second section provides guidance and establishes independence standards for auditors conducting financial audits, attestation engagements, reviews of financial statements, and performance audits under GAGAS. This section highlights the importance of independence to the auditor and the audit organization. The third section establishes the standard for the auditor's use of professional judgment and provides related application guidance.

> The requirements in chapter 3 of the Yellow Book are intended to be followed in conjunction with all other applicable GAGAS requirements.

Ethical principles

The ethical principles of GAGAS provide the foundation, discipline, and structure, as well as the environment, that influence the application of GAGAS.

Because auditing is one of the cornerstones of government accountability to the public, a strong foundation of ethical principles is expected of all audit organizations and auditors who conduct their work in accordance with GAGAS. An essential element of a positive ethical environment is the ethical tone maintained and demonstrated by management and staff of the audit organization. Management sets the tone for ethical behavior throughout the organization by maintaining an ethical culture, clearly communicating acceptable behavior and expectations to each employee, and creating an environment that reinforces and encourages ethical behavior throughout all levels of the organization.

Performing audit work in accordance with ethical principles is a matter of personal and organizational responsibility. Ethical principles apply in

- preserving auditor independence,
- taking on only work that the auditor is competent to perform,
- performing high-quality work, and
- following the applicable standards cited in the audit report.

When auditors perform their work and make decisions that are consistent with the broader interest of those relying on the auditors' report, including the public, then integrity and objectivity are maintained.

Auditors who conduct audits in accordance with GAGAS may also be subject to other ethical requirements or codes of professional conduct. For instance, many professional organizations or bodies that license or certify professionals may also impose ethical requirements on individual auditors who are members of those organizations or licensing bodies. Auditors in governmental entities may also be subject to government ethics laws and regulations.

The work of auditors who conduct audits in accordance with GAGAS is guided by the following ethical principles:

- The public interest
- Integrity
- Objectivity
- Proper use of government information, resources, and positions
- Professional behavior

The public interest

The collective well-being of the community of people and entities that the auditors serve is characterized as the "public interest." Auditors best serve the public interest and honor the public trust by observing integrity, objectivity, and independence in discharging their professional responsibilities. The principle of the public interest is fundamental to the responsibilities of auditors and critical in the government environment.

A distinguishing mark of an auditor is the acceptance of responsibility to serve the public interest. When auditing in the government environment, the responsibility to service the public interest is critical. GAGAS embodies the concept of accountability for public resources, which is fundamental to serving the public interest.

Integrity

Auditors performing their professional responsibilities with integrity maintain and strengthen the public's confidence in government. Auditors performing their work with an attitude that is objective, fact-based, nonpartisan, and nonideological with regard to audited entities and users of the audit reports are cornerstones of the principle of integrity. Communication with the audited entity, those charged with governance, and the individuals contracting for or requesting the engagement are expected to be honest, candid, and constructive within the constraints of applicable confidentiality laws, regulations, or policies.

Additionally, the principle of integrity encompasses auditors making decisions consistent with the public interest of the program or activity under audit. In discharging their professional responsibilities, auditors may encounter conflicting pressures from management of the audited entity, various levels of government, and other likely users. Furthermore, auditors may encounter pressures to inappropriately achieve personal or organizational gain. Acting with integrity means that auditors place priority on their responsibilities to the public interest when responding to those conflicts and pressures.

Objectivity

The credibility of auditing in the government sector is based on auditors' objectivity in discharging their professional responsibilities. Objectivity includes being independent of mind and appearance when conducting engagements, maintaining an attitude of impartiality, having intellectual honesty, and being free of conflicts of interest. Maintaining objectivity includes a continuing assessment of relationships with audited entities and other stakeholders in the context of the auditor's responsibility to the public. The concepts of objectivity and independence are closely related. Independence impairments affect objectivity.

Proper use of government information, resources, and positions

Government information, resources, and positions

- are to be used for official purposes only.
- are not to be used for the auditor's personal gain.
- are not to be used in a manner contrary to law or detrimental to the legitimate interests of the audited entity or the audit organization.

This concept also includes the proper handling of sensitive or classified information or resources.

The public's right to the transparency of government information has to be weighed against with the proper use of that information in the government environment. In addition, many government programs are subject to laws and regulations dealing with the disclosure of information. A critical part of achieving this balance is by auditors exercising discretion when using information acquired in the course of their professional responsibilities. It is not appropriate to improperly disclose any such information to third parties.

An essential part of auditors' responsibilities is to be accountable to the public for the proper use and prudent management of government resources. The public expects auditors to protect and conserve government resources and to use them appropriately for authorized purposes.

Misusing the auditor position for financial gain or other benefits violates an auditor's fundamental responsibilities. An auditor's credibility can be damaged by actions that could be perceived by an objective third party with knowledge of the relevant information as improperly benefiting an auditor's personal financial interests or those of

- an immediate or close family member;
- a general partner;
- an entity for which the auditor serves as an officer, director, trustee, or employee; or
- an entity with which the auditor is negotiating concerning future employment.

Professional behavior

The public has high expectations for the auditing profession. It is essential that auditors comply with all relevant legal, regulatory, and professional obligations. With this objective in mind, auditors should exhibit appropriate professional behavior by avoiding any conduct that could bring discredit to auditors' work, including actions that would cause an objective third party with knowledge of the relevant information to conclude that the auditors' work was professionally deficient. Professional behavior includes auditors putting forth an honest effort in performing their duties in accordance with the relevant technical and professional standards.

Knowledge check

1. In GAGAS audits, which ethical principle includes an auditor being independent of mind and appearance when providing audit and attestation engagements?

    a. The public interest.
    b. Objectivity.
    c. Professional behavior.
    d. Proper use of government information, resources, and position.

Independence

The consideration of independence in a single audit is a critical one — one that has been found to be frequently deficient based on peer reviews and federal agency reviews. This chapter will not only provide GAGAS requirements, but also highlight areas frequently misunderstood or misinterpreted. Keep in mind that the GAGAS requirements regarding independence that an auditor is required to follow may be different from other independence requirements for an auditor — for example, the AICPA Code of Professional Conduct.

GAGAS's practical consideration of independence consists of four interrelated sections, as follows:

- General requirements and application guidance
- Requirements for and guidance on a conceptual framework for making independence determinations based on facts and circumstances that are often unique to specific environments
- Requirements for and guidance on independence for auditors providing nonaudit services, including identification of specific nonaudit services that
  - always impair independence
  - create threats
  - would not normally impair independence
- Requirements for and guidance on documentation necessary to support adequate consideration of auditor independence

Paragraphs 3.18–3.20 of GAGAS	Requirements: Independence - General
	3.18 In all matters relating to the GAGAS engagement, auditors and audit organizations must be independent from an audited entity.
	3.19 Auditors and audit organizations should avoid situations that could lead reasonable and informed third parties to conclude that the auditors and audit organizations are not independent and thus are not capable of exercising objective and impartial judgment on all issues associated with conducting the engagement and reporting on the work.
	3.20 Except under the limited circumstances discussed in paragraphs 3.66 and 3.67, auditors and audit organizations should be independent from an audited entity during *a.* any period of time that falls within the period covered by the financial statements or subject matter of the engagement and *b.* the period of professional engagement.

What is independence under GAGAS?

Independence has two components; independence of mind and independence of appearance.

Independence of mind

> The state of mind that permits the conduct of an engagement without being affected by influences that compromise professional judgment, thereby allowing an individual to act with integrity and exercise objectivity and professional skepticism.

Independence in appearance

> The absence of circumstances that would cause a reasonable and informed third party to reasonably conclude that the integrity, objectivity, or professional skepticism of an audit organization or member of the engagement team had been compromised.

Auditors and audit organizations must maintain independence so that their opinions, findings, conclusions, judgments, and recommendations will be impartial and viewed as impartial by reasonable and informed third parties. Both independence of mind and independence in appearance are important in maintaining auditor independence.

When should the auditor be independent?

In an engagement conducted in accordance with GAGAS, except in very limited circumstances, auditors should be independent from an audited entity during

- any period of time that falls within the period covered by the financial statements or subject matter of the engagement, and
- the period of professional engagement.

The period of professional engagement begins when auditors either (1) sign an initial engagement letter or other agreement to conduct an engagement or (2) begin to conduct an engagement, whichever is earlier. Note that the period of professional engagement does not necessarily end with the issuance of a report and recommence with the beginning of the following year's engagement or a subsequent engagement with a similar objective. Instead, the period lasts for the duration of the professional relationship — which, for recurring engagements, could cover many periods or years. The relationship would be considered completed when either formal or informal communication is made of termination by the auditors or the audited entity or with the issuance of a report, whichever is later.

> The 2018 Yellow Book is effective for audits of fiscal years ending on or after June 30, 2020. Therefore, auditors are required to comply with the 2018 Yellow Book independence standard beginning July 1, 2019, for a June 30, 2020, year-end audit.

GAGAS conceptual framework approach to independence

In order to consider the many different circumstances, or combinations of circumstances, relevant to evaluating threats to independence, GAGAS establishes a conceptual framework that auditors use to identify, evaluate, and apply safeguards to address threats to independence.

The conceptual framework assists auditors in maintaining both independence of mind and independence in appearance. It allows auditors to address threats to independence that result from activities that are not specifically prohibited by GAGAS. Figure 1 of GAGAS chapter 3 is a good resource for auditors when assessing independence and evaluating whether all requirements related to that assessment have been adequately considered.

Paragraphs 3.27–3.34 of GAGAS	Requirements: GAGAS Conceptual Framework Approach to Independence
	3.27 Auditors should apply the conceptual framework at the audit organization, engagement team, and individual auditor levels to a. identify threats to independence; b. evaluate the significance of the threats identified, both individually and in the aggregate; and c. apply safeguards as necessary to eliminate the threats or reduce them to an acceptable level. **3.28** Auditors should reevaluate threats to independence, including any safeguards applied, whenever the audit organization or the auditors become aware of new information or changes in facts and circumstances that could affect whether a threat has been eliminated or reduced to an acceptable level. **3.29** Auditors should use professional judgment when applying the conceptual framework. **3.30** Auditors should evaluate the following broad categories of threats to independence when applying the GAGAS conceptual framework: a. Self-interest threat: The threat that a financial or other interest will inappropriately influence an auditor's judgment or behavior. b. Self-review threat: The threat that an auditor or audit organization that has provided nonaudit services will not appropriately evaluate the results of previous judgments made or services provided as part of the nonaudit services when forming a judgment significant to a GAGAS engagement. c. Bias threat: The threat that an auditor will, as a result of political, ideological, social, or other convictions, take a position that is not objective.

d. Familiarity threat: The threat that aspects of a relationship with management or personnel of an audited entity, such as a close or long relationship, or that of an immediate or close family member, will lead an auditor to take a position that is not objective.

e. Undue influence threat: The threat that influences or pressures from sources external to the audit organization will affect an auditor's ability to make objective judgments.

f. Management participation threat: The threat that results from an auditor's taking on the role of management or otherwise performing management functions on behalf of the audited entity, which will lead an auditor to take a position that is not objective.

g. Structural threat: The threat that an audit organization's placement within a government entity, in combination with the structure of the government entity being audited, will affect the audit organization's ability to perform work and report results objectively.

3.31 Auditors should determine whether identified threats to independence are at an acceptable level or have been eliminated or reduced to an acceptable level, considering both qualitative and quantitative factors to determine the significance of a threat.

3.32 When auditors determine that threats to independence are not at an acceptable level, the auditors should determine whether appropriate safeguards can be applied to eliminate the threats or reduce them to an acceptable level.

3.33 In cases where auditors determine that threats to independence require the application of safeguards, auditors should document the threats identified and the safeguards applied to eliminate or reduce the threats to an acceptable level.

3.34 If auditors initially identify a threat to independence after the audit report is issued, auditors should evaluate the threat's effect on the engagement and on GAGAS compliance. If the auditors determine that the newly identified threat's effect on the engagement would have resulted in the audit report being different from the report issued had the auditors been aware of it, they should communicate in the same manner as that used to originally distribute the report to those charged with governance, the appropriate officials of the audited entity, the appropriate officials of the audit organization requiring or arranging for the engagements, and other known users, so that they do not continue to rely on findings or conclusions that were affected by the threat to independence. If auditors previously posted the report to their publicly accessible website, they should remove the report and post a public notification that the report was removed. The auditors should then determine whether to perform the additional engagement work necessary to reissue the report, including any revised findings or conclusions, or to repost the original report if the additional engagement work does not result in a change in findings or conclusions.

Offices or units of an audit organization or related or affiliated entities under common control are not differentiated from one another as it relates to the consideration of auditor independence. Accordingly, when evaluating independence using the conceptual framework, an audit organization that includes multiple offices or units — or includes multiple entities related or affiliated through common control — is considered to be one audit organization. However, common ownership may affect independence in appearance regardless of the level of control.

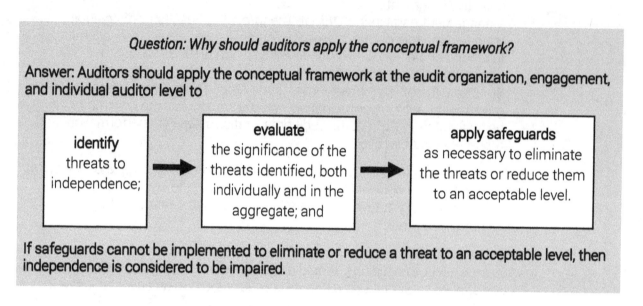

Question: Why should auditors apply the conceptual framework?

Answer: Auditors should apply the conceptual framework at the audit organization, engagement, and individual auditor level to

| **identify** threats to independence; | → | **evaluate** the significance of the threats identified, both individually and in the aggregate; and | → | **apply safeguards** as necessary to eliminate the threats or reduce them to an acceptable level. |

If safeguards cannot be implemented to eliminate or reduce a threat to an acceptable level, then independence is considered to be impaired.

Identifying and evaluating threats to independence

The start of a new engagement, assignment of new personnel to an ongoing engagement, and acceptance of a nonaudit service for an audited entity are some of the facts and circumstances that create threats to independence. Threats to independence also may be created by a wide range of relationships and circumstances. A threat to independence in one of the categories set forth in GAGAS may result in other threats as well.

Threats to independence are assessed to determine whether identified threats to independence are at an acceptable level or have been eliminated or reduced to an acceptable level. Both qualitative and quantitative factors should be evaluated to determine the significance of a threat.

An acceptable level is defined by GAGAS as the level at which a reasonable and informed third party would likely conclude that the audit organization or auditor is independent. The concept of a reasonable and informed third party is a test that involves an evaluation by a hypothetical person. Such a person possesses skills, knowledge, and experience to objectively evaluate the appropriateness of the auditor's judgments and conclusions. This evaluation entails weighing all the relevant facts and circumstances, including any safeguards applied, that the auditor knows, or could reasonably be expected to know, at the time that the evaluation is made a threat to independence is not at an acceptable level if it could either

- affect the auditors' ability to conduct an engagement without being affected by influences that compromise professional judgment or
- expose the auditors or audit organization to circumstances that would cause a reasonable and informed third party to conclude that the integrity, objectivity, or professional skepticism of the audit organization, or an auditor, had been compromised.

The 2018 Yellow Book clarifies that threats to independence should be reevaluated during the course of the audit, because circumstances may change or the auditor may become aware of new information. Because threats can have a cumulative effect on auditors' independence, threats to independence are evaluated both individually and in the aggregate.

As discussed later in this chapter, GAGAS specifically addresses threats related to nonaudit services provided by audit organizations, and includes requirements and guidance on evaluating threats to independence related to nonaudit services.

Examples of threats to independence

GAGAS provides a number of examples of threats to independence in the various broad categories as follows:

Self-interest threats	Self-review threats	Bias threats	Familiarity threats
• An audit organization having undue dependence on income from a particular audited entity. • A member of the audit team entering into employment negotiations with an audited entity. • An audit organization discovering a significant error when evaluating the results of a previous professional service provided by the audit organization. • A member of the audit team having a direct financial interest in the audited entity. This would not, however, preclude auditors from auditing pension plans that they participate in if (1) the auditors have no control over the investment strategy, benefits, or other management issues associated with the pension plan and (2) the auditors belong to such pension plan as part of their employment with the audit organization or prior employment with the audited entity, provided that the plan is normally offered to all employees in equivalent employment positions.	• An audit organization issuing a report on the effectiveness of the operation of financial or performance management systems after designing or implementing the systems. • An audit organization having prepared the original data used to generate records that are the subject matter of the engagement. • An audit organization providing a service for an audited entity that directly affects the subject matter information of the engagement. • A member of the engagement team being, or having recently been, employed by the audited entity in a position to exert significant influence over the subject matter of the engagement.	• A member of the engagement team having preconceptions about the objectives of a program under audit that are strong enough to affect the auditor's objectivity. • A member of the engagement team having biases associated with political, ideological, or social convictions that result from membership or employment in, or loyalty to, a particular type of policy, group, entity, or level of government that could affect the auditor's objectivity.	• A member of the engagement team having a close or immediate family member who is a principal or senior manager of the audited entity. • A member of the engagement team having a close or immediate family member who is an employee of the audited entity and is in a position to exert significant influence over the subject matter of the engagement. • A principal or employee of the audited entity having recently served on the engagement team in a position to exert significant influence over the subject matter of the engagement. • An auditor accepting gifts or preferential treatment from an audited entity, unless the value is trivial or inconsequential. • Senior engagement personnel having a long association with the audited entity.

Undue influence threats	Management participation threats	Structural threats
• External interference or influence that could improperly limit or modify the scope of an engagement or threaten to do so, including exerting pressure to inappropriately reduce the extent of work performed in order to reduce costs or fees. • External interference with the selection or application of engagement procedures or in the selection of transactions to be examined. • Unreasonable restrictions on the time allowed to complete an engagement or issue the report. • External interference over assignment, appointment, compensation, and promotion. • Restrictions on funds or other resources provided to the audit organization that adversely affect the audit organization's ability to carry out its responsibilities. • Authority to overrule or to inappropriately influence the auditors' judgment as to the appropriate content of the report. • Threat of replacing the auditor or the audit organization based on a disagreement with the contents of an audit report, the auditors' conclusions, or the application of an accounting principle or other criteria. • Influences that jeopardize the auditors' continued employment for reasons other than incompetence, misconduct, or the audited entity's need for GAGAS engagements.	• A member of the engagement team being, or having recently been, a principal or senior manager of the audited entity. • An auditor serving as a voting member of an entity's management committee or board of directors, making policy decisions that affect future direction and operation of an entity's programs, supervising entity employees, developing or approving programmatic policy, authorizing an entity's transactions, or maintaining custody of an entity's assets. • An auditor or audit organization recommending a single individual for a specific position that is key to the audited entity or program under audit, or otherwise ranking or influencing management's selection of the candidate.	• For both external and internal audit organizations, structural placement of the audit function within the reporting line of the areas under audit. • For internal audit organizations, administrative direction from the audited entity's management.

Applying safeguards

Safeguards play an important part when evaluating whether a threat impairs the auditor's independence. *Safeguards* are actions or other measures, individually or in combination, that auditors and audit organizations take that effectively eliminate threats to independence or reduce them to an acceptable level.

Clear identification of a specific threat is needed in order to identify an effective safeguard to apply to that threat. Furthermore, an applied safeguard not only has to be effective, but also needs to be implemented. Safeguards vary depending on the facts and circumstances. Examples of safeguards include the following:

- Consulting an independent third party — such as a professional organization, a professional regulatory body, or another auditor — to discuss engagement issues or assess issues that are highly technical or require significant judgment;
- Involving another audit organization to perform or reperform part of the engagement;
- Having an auditor who was not a member of the engagement team review the work performed;
- Removing an auditor from an engagement team when that auditor's financial or other interests or relationships pose a threat to independence.

The safeguards noted here are not appropriate for all circumstances though they can provide a starting point for auditors who have identified threats to independence and are considering what safeguards could eliminate those threats or reduce them to an acceptable level. In some cases, multiple safeguards may be necessary to address a threat. Additionally, there may be some threats that are so significant that there are no safeguards that can be effectively applied to adequately eliminate or reduce them to an acceptable level. Note that examples of safeguards specifically related to nonaudit services are covered later in this chapter.

Independence impairments

Paragraphs 3.59–3.60 of GAGAS	Requirements: Independence Impairments
	3.59 Auditors should conclude that independence is impaired if no safeguards have been effectively applied to eliminate an unacceptable threat or reduce it to an acceptable level.
	3.60 When auditors conclude that independence of the engagement team or the audit organization is impaired under paragraph 3.59, auditors should decline to accept an engagement or should terminate an engagement in progress (except in circumstances discussed in paragraphs 3.25 or 3.84).

The determination of whether independence is impaired depends on

- the nature of the threat,
- whether the threat is of such significance that it would compromise an auditor's professional judgment or create the appearance that the auditor's integrity, objectivity, or professional skepticism may be compromised, and
- the specific safeguards applied to eliminate the threat or reduce it to an acceptable level.

If auditors conclude that an individual auditor's independence is impaired, it may be necessary to terminate the engagement if actions are not available to address the effect of the individual auditor's independence impairment.

> There are some nonaudit services expressly prohibited by GAGAS. Per GAGAS, there are no safeguards available that would mitigate the threat to independence those nonaudit services create. These prohibited services are found throughout the GAGAS requirements.

> Factors that are relevant in evaluating whether the independence of the engagement team or the audit organization is impaired by an individual auditor's independence impairment include the following:
> - The nature and duration of the individual auditor's impairment
> - The number and nature of any previous impairments with respect to the current engagement
> - Whether a member of the engagement team had knowledge of the interest or relationship that caused the individual auditor's impairment
> - Whether the individual auditor whose independence is impaired is (1) a member of the engagement team or (2) another individual for whom there are independence requirements
> - The role of the individual auditor on the engagement team whose independence is impaired
> - The effect of the service, if any, on the accounting records or audited entity's financial statements if the individual auditor's impairment was caused by the provision of a nonaudit service
> - Whether a partner or director of the audit organization had knowledge of the individual auditor's impairment and failed to ensure that the individual auditor's impairment was promptly communicated to an appropriate individual within the audit organization
> - The extent of the self-interest, undue influence, or other threats created by the individual auditor's impairment

Figure 1: GAGAS conceptual framework for independence

Figure 1 in chapter 3 of the 2018 Yellow Book includes the following flowchart to assist auditors in the application of the conceptual framework for independence. (Note: Figure 2, referenced in Figure 1, is presented later in this chapter.)

safeguards applied

Source: GAO. | GAO-18-568G

Knowledge check

2. Under GAGAS, all of the following are a category of threats **except**

    a. A bias threat.
    b. A documentation threat.
    c. An undue influence threat.
    d. A structural threat.

3. Under GAGAS, the threat that external influences or pressures will affect an auditor's ability to make objective judgments is

    a. A management participation threat.
    b. A structural threat.
    c. A bias threat.
    d. An undue influence threat.

4. Auditors apply the conceptual framework of GAGAS to do all **except**

    a. Document the understanding with the audited entity.
    b. Apply safeguards as necessary.
    c. Identify threats to independence.
    d. Evaluate the significance of threats identified.

Case study 3-1: Evaluation of threats and safeguards

WASS CPAs is a local firm with four partners:

- Maggie Winter, CPA (tax and audit partner)
- Melissa Autumn, CPA (audit partner)
- Francine Spring, CPA (audit partner)
- Annette Summer, CPA (tax and quality control partner)

WASS has 45 other staff members, 29 of which are CPAs. The staff is used for audit, tax, and other client services. It is now September and Melissa is sitting in her office pondering the winter audit season. Her partners — Maggie, Annette, and Francine, are finalizing their June 30 audits, and the staff is busy getting ready to plan the upcoming December 31 audits.

The following situations have Melissa concerned, and she is considering the potential threats and possible safeguards that the firm may impose to continue performing WASS's audits.

Situation 1: Peter Doright, CPA and manager, has been approached by Trailblazer Adventure Group to become the new chief financial officer when the current person retires in May of next year. He is scheduled to manage the audit for the fiscal year ending this December 31 and the audit should be completed by the end of March. She is not sure whether Peter is considering taking the position.

Situation 2: John Whyling, who is a CPA and has been hired by the firm as a senior staff member, just started with the firm this past June. John joined WASS after his work with a government audit client of WASS (the

City of Urlaub), where he was a staff accountant. His responsibilities with City of Urlaub included purchase order processing and reconciling bank statements. John also assisted in posting journal entries to the general ledger software. The staffing personnel at WASS have assigned John to the engagement team on the City of Urlaub's audit this year with the fiscal year ending December 31.

Situation 3: Tom Hinterspot is a non-CPA staff assistant at PMM. Tom has become active in the local Libertarian Party and is campaigning for some of the local politicians running for office. Additionally, some of these politicians, if elected, would hold office with WASS's government clients.

Situation 4: Francine Spring, CPA, and an audit partner with WASS, has worked as the in-charge partner for the past 20 years on the Service Animals for the Elderly not-for-profit engagement. Service Animals for the Elderly is associated with the Episcopal diocese of the area (Francine is Episcopal). She has served on some ad hoc committees for the bishop of the diocese over the past two years. Francine's three grown children graduated from Episcopal schools.

Situation 5: Care for Coyotes, Inc. has changed the audit completion date from March 29, 20x1 to February 22, 20x1. This scheduling change reduces the engagement time (based on former audits for the client) by five weeks. There is a question: Will WASS staffing be able to provide enough personnel to complete the audit?

Situation 6: Maggie Winter, a CPA and partner for both tax and audit, has recently been asked to serve on the board of trustees for Advocating Hope Community College (an audit client with a June 30 fiscal year-end). She has indicated that she would like to be a trustee but wanted the partners to agree with her decision. She was also informed that the manager on the audit, Jennifer Kapplinger (also a CPA) has been asked to serve on an ad hoc committee that will review the business department's curriculum and make some recommendations to the board of trustees as to the future direction of the department.

Situation 7: The Saving Grace Medical Institute has been a client of WASS for the last 30 years. The institute has grown to an international organization and, as a result, the engagement demands a great deal of staff and time to complete each year. Thank goodness, this client has a March 31 year-end, which permits the firm to perform a majority of the work between the end of tax season and before the June 30 year-end audit begins. The institute's fees represent approximately 35% of WASS's gross income for the partnership. If WASS loses this client, Melissa wonders how WASS will support its overhead and maintain current staffing levels.

Case study

For each of the seven situations, help Melissa Autumn decide whether potential threats do exist and if so, which type of threat is present. Additionally, help her determine whether the threats are significant, and whether safeguards can be put into place to overcome identified threats to independence.

Providing nonaudit services to audited entities

Auditors have traditionally provided a range of nonaudit services that are consistent with their skills and expertise. However, when providing these nonaudit services to audited entities, auditors need to consider that these services may create threats to the independence of auditors or audit organizations. Auditors may be able to provide nonaudit services without impairing independence if

- the nonaudit services are not expressly prohibited by GAGAS,
- the auditors have determined that the requirements for providing nonaudit services have been met, and
- any significant threats to independence have been eliminated or reduced to an acceptable level.

The conceptual framework enables auditors to evaluate independence given the facts and circumstances of individual services that are not specifically prohibited.

Paragraph 3.64 of GAGAS	Requirement: Nonaudit Services
	3.64 Before auditors agree to provide a nonaudit service to an audited entity, they should determine whether providing such a service would create a threat to independence, either by itself or in aggregate with other nonaudit services provided, with respect to any GAGAS engagement they conduct.

Considerations related to the evaluation of nonaudit services

For financial audits, examination or review engagements, and reviews of financial statements, a nonaudit service otherwise prohibited by GAGAS and provided during the period covered by the financial statements may not threaten independence with respect to those financial statements provided that the following conditions exist:

- The nonaudit service was provided prior to the period of professional engagement
- The nonaudit service related only to periods prior to the period covered by the financial statements
- The financial statements for the period to which the nonaudit service did relate were audited by other auditors

Auditors should be aware that nonaudit services provided can affect independence of mind and in appearance in periods after the nonaudit services were provided. A good example is if auditors have designed and implemented an accounting and financial reporting system that is expected to be in place for many years. Such a service could create a threat to independence in appearance for future engagements that those auditors conduct. For recurring engagements, an effective safeguard that allows the audit organization that provided such a nonaudit service to mitigate the independence threat may be to have another independent audit organization conduct an engagement over the areas affected by the nonaudit service. For performance audits and agreed-upon procedures engagements, nonaudit services that are otherwise prohibited by GAGAS may be provided when such services do not relate to the specific subject matter of the engagement.

Routine activities

> Routine activities that auditors perform related directly to conducting an engagement, such as providing advice and responding to questions as part of an engagement, are not considered nonaudit services under GAGAS.

Routine activities generally involve providing advice or assistance to the audited entity on an informal basis as part of an engagement, and typically involve an insignificant amount of time incurred or resources. They generally do not result in a specific project or engagement or in the auditors producing a formal report or other formal work product.

However, activities such as financial statement preparation, cash-to-accrual conversions, and reconciliations are considered nonaudit services under GAGAS — not routine activities related to the performance of an engagement — and are evaluated using the conceptual framework.

Routine activities directly related to an engagement may include the following:

- Providing advice to the audited entity on an accounting matter as an ancillary part of the overall financial audit
- Providing advice to the audited entity on routine business matters
- Educating the audited entity about matters within the technical expertise of the auditors
- Providing information to the audited entity that is readily available to the auditors, such as best practices and benchmarking studies

Safeguards related to nonaudit services

> **Examples of possible safeguards in addressing threats to independence related to nonaudit services**
>
> - Not including individuals who provided the nonaudit service as engagement team members
> - Having another auditor, not associated with the engagement, review the engagement and nonaudit work as appropriate
> - Engaging another audit organization to evaluate the results of the nonaudit service
> - Having another audit organization reperform the nonaudit service to the extent necessary to enable that other audit organization to take responsibility for the service

Management responsibilities

Paragraphs 3.73–3.78 of GAGAS	Requirements: Nonaudit Services

Requirements: Nonaudit Services

3.73 Before auditors agree to provide nonaudit services to an audited entity that the audited entity's management requested and that could create a threat to independence, either by themselves or in aggregate with other nonaudit services provided, with respect to any GAGAS engagement they conduct, auditors should determine that the audited entity has designated an individual who possesses suitable skill, knowledge, or experience and that the individual understands the services to be provided sufficiently to oversee them.

3.74 Auditors should document consideration of management's ability to effectively oversee nonaudit services to be provided.

3.75 In cases where the audited entity is unable or unwilling to assume these responsibilities (for example, the audited entity does not have an individual with suitable skill, knowledge, or experience to oversee the nonaudit services provided, or is unwilling to perform such functions because of lack of time or desire), auditors should conclude that the provision of these services is an impairment to independence.

3.76 Auditors providing nonaudit services to audited entities should obtain agreement from audited entity management that audited entity management performs the following functions in connection with the nonaudit services:

a. assumes all management responsibilities;
b. oversees the services, by designating an individual, preferably within senior management, who possesses suitable skill, knowledge, or experience;
c. evaluates the adequacy and results of the services provided; and
d. accepts responsibility for the results of the services.

3.77 In connection with nonaudit services, auditors should establish and document their understanding with the audited entity's management or those charged with governance, as appropriate, regarding the following:

a. objectives of the nonaudit service,
b. services to be provided,
c. audited entity's acceptance of its responsibilities as discussed in paragraph 3.76,
d. the auditors' responsibilities, and
e. any limitations on the provision of nonaudit services.

3.78 Auditors should conclude that management responsibilities that the auditors perform for an audited entity are impairments to independence. If the auditors were to assume management responsibilities for an audited entity, the management participation threats created would be so significant that no safeguards could reduce them to an acceptable level.

Consideration of management's ability to effectively oversee the nonaudit service to be provided is a critical component of determining whether a threat to independence exists. Although the responsible individual in management is required to have sufficient expertise to oversee the nonaudit services, management is not required to possess the expertise to perform or reperform the services.

> Indicators of management's ability to effectively oversee a nonaudit service include management's ability to determine the reasonableness of the results of the nonaudit services provided, and to recognize a material error, omission, or misstatement in the results of the nonaudit services provided.

The auditor should determine that the auditee has designated a suitable individual with skill, knowledge, and experience prior to agreeing to provide a nonaudit service. As illustrated in figure 1 of chapter 3, GAGAS specifies that this determination is essential to the auditors assessment that a nonaudit service does not impair independence. When auditee management is unable or unwilling to designate an individual to oversee a nonaudit service, independence is considered to be impaired. Consequently, an auditee designating an individual with suitable skill, knowledge, and experience would not be a consideration when determining safeguards that could be applied to a threat to independence.

Management responsibilities that impair independence

Management responsibilities involve leading and directing an entity, including making decisions regarding the acquisition, deployment, and control of human, financial, physical, and intangible resources. The following box lists examples of management responsibilities; however, whether a specific activity is a management responsibility or otherwise depends on the facts and circumstances. It is important to note that if auditors were to assume management responsibilities for an audited entity, the management participation threat created would be so significant that no safeguard could reduce them to an acceptable level.

> ### Examples of management responsibilities
>
> - Setting policies and strategic direction for the audited entity
> - Directing and accepting responsibility for the actions of the audited entity's employees in the performance of their routine, recurring activities
> - Having custody of an audited entity's assets
> - Reporting to those charged with governance on behalf of management
> - Deciding which of the audit organization's or outside third party's recommendations to implement
> - Accepting responsibility for the management of an audited entity's project
> - Accepting responsibility for designing, implementing, or maintaining internal control
> - Providing services that are intended to be used as management's primary basis for making decisions that are significant to the subject matter of the engagement
> - Developing an audited entity's performance measurement system when that system is material or significant to the subject matter of the engagement
> - Serving as a voting member of an audited entity's management committee or board of directors

Paragraphs 3.83–3.84 of GAGAS	Requirements: Providing Nonaudit Services
	3.83 Auditors who previously provided nonaudit services for an entity that is a prospective subject of an engagement should evaluate the effect of those nonaudit services on independence before agreeing to conduct a GAGAS engagement. If auditors provided a nonaudit service in the period to be covered by the engagement, they should (1) determine if GAGAS expressly prohibits the nonaudit service; (2) if audited entity management requested the nonaudit service, determine whether the skills, knowledge, and experience of the individual responsible for overseeing the nonaudit service were sufficient; and (3) determine whether a threat to independence exists and address any threats noted in accordance with the conceptual framework.
	3.84 Auditors in a government entity may be required to provide a nonaudit service that impairs the auditors' independence with respect to a required engagement. If, because of constitutional or statutory requirements over which they have no control, the auditors can neither implement safeguards to reduce the resulting threat to an acceptable level nor decline to provide or terminate a nonaudit service that is incompatible with engagement responsibilities, auditors should disclose the nature of the threat that could not be eliminated or reduced to an acceptable level and modify the GAGAS compliance statement as discussed in paragraph 2.17b accordingly. Determining how to modify the GAGAS compliance statement in these circumstances is a matter of professional judgment.

Knowledge check

5. Under the Yellow Book, all of the following examples of safeguards help eliminate threats to auditor independence, **except**

    a. Not including individuals who provided the nonaudit service as engagement team members.
    b. Engaging another audit organization to evaluate the results of the nonaudit service.
    c. Having another auditor, not associated with the engagement, review the engagement and nonaudit work performed.
    d. Retaining an individual on an audit team when that individual's financial or other interests or relationships pose a threat to independence.

6. Activities that would be considered a management responsibility, and therefore would impair independence, include all of the following **except**

    a. Deciding which recommendations of the auditor or outside third party to implement.
    b. Providing advice to the audited entity on routine business matters.
    c. Having custody of the audited entity assets.
    d. Setting policies and strategic direction for the audited entity.

Consideration of specific nonaudit services

The 2018 Yellow Book provides information on independence as it relates to nonaudit services. Some activities in the categories noted here impair independence because, by their nature, they support the entity's operations; however, auditors may be able to provide nonaudit services in these categories without impairing independence if

- the nonaudit services are not expressly prohibited by GAGAS,
- the auditors have determined that the requirements for providing the nonaudit services have been met, and
- any significant threats to independence have been eliminated or reduced to an acceptable level through the application of safeguards.

The GAGAS conceptual framework enables auditors to evaluate independence as it relates to nonaudit services not expressly prohibited.

Nonaudit services expressly prohibited in GAGAS are found in the following areas:

- Preparing accounting records and financial statements
- Internal audit assistance services provided by external auditors
- Internal control evaluation as a nonaudit service
- Information technology services
- Appraisal, valuation and actuarial services
- Other nonaudit services including the following:
  - Advisory service
  - Benefit plan administration
  - Business risk consulting
  - Executive or employee recruiting
  - Investment advisory or management

Preparing accounting records and financial statements

The 2018 Yellow Book provides guidance regarding specific nonaudit services related to preparing accounting records and financial statements. Certain of those types of nonaudit services impair independence as there are no safeguards sufficient to eliminate or mitigate the threat to an acceptable level. Others are determined to be significant threats, which may be performed only if safeguards are available to eliminate the threats or reduce them to an acceptable level. Finally, certain nonaudit services related to preparing accounting records and preparing financial statements are specifically identified as being threats to the auditor's independence. For those nonaudit services, the auditor needs to evaluate the threat to determine if it is a significant threat and document that evaluation. The auditor then proceeds depending on whether a threat or significant threat has been identified.

Figure 2 in chapter 3 of GAGAS provides a decision tree that assists in the independence considerations for preparing records and financial statements for those services not expressly prohibited by GAGAS.

Paragraphs 3.87–3.90 of GAGAS	Requirements: Preparing Accounting Records and Financial Statements
	3.87 Auditors should conclude that the following services involving preparation of accounting records impair independence with respect to an audited entity:
	a. determining or changing journal entries, account codes or classifications for transactions, or other accounting records for the entity without obtaining management's approval;
	b. authorizing or approving the entity's transactions; and
	c. preparing or making changes to source documents without management approval.
	3.88 Auditors should conclude that preparing financial statements in their entirety from a client-provided trial balance or underlying accounting records creates significant threats to auditors' independence and should document the threats and safeguards applied to eliminate and reduce threats to an acceptable level in accordance with paragraph 3.33 or decline to provide the services.
	3.89 Auditors should identify as threats to independence any services related to preparing accounting records and financial statements, other than those defined as impairments to independence in paragraph 3.87 and significant threats in paragraph 3.88. These services include
	a. recording transactions for which management has determined or approved the appropriate account classification, or posting coded transactions to an audited entity's general ledger;
	b. preparing certain line items or sections of the financial statements based on information in the trial balance;
	c. posting entries that an audited entity's management has approved to the entity's trial balance; and
	d. preparing account reconciliations that identify reconciling items for the audited entity management's evaluation.
	3.90 Auditors should evaluate the significance of threats to independence created by providing any services discussed in paragraph 3.89 and should document the evaluation of the significance of such threats.

Management must take responsibility for the preparation and fair presentation of the financial statements in accordance with the applicable financial reporting framework. This is the case even if the auditor assisted in drafting the financial statements. Consequently, an auditor who accepts responsibility for the preparation and fair presentation of financial statements that the auditor will subsequently audit, or that will otherwise be the subject matter of an engagement, would impair the auditor's independence.

Source documents include those providing evidence that the transaction occurred, such as purchase orders, payroll time records, customer orders, and contracts. Additionally, records include an audited entity's general ledger and subsidiary records or the equivalent. Preparing or making changes to these types of source documents without management's approval would impair independence.

Professional judgment is needed when determining whether services performed are significant threats that require safeguards. Clerical assistance, such as typing, formatting, printing, and binding financial statements is not typically considered a significant threat.

Factors to consider when determining the significance of any threats created by the audit organization preparing accounting records and financial statements as a nonaudit service include:

- The extent to which the outcome of the service could have a material effect on the financial statements
- The degree of subjectivity involved in determining the appropriate amounts or treatment for those matters reflected in the financial statements
- The extent of the audited entity's involvement in determining significant matters of judgment

GAGAS provides a flowchart to assist auditors in the independence considerations for preparing accounting records and financial statements. This flowchart is used for services not expressly prohibited by GAGAS.

Figure 2: Independence Consideration for Preparing Accounting Records and Financial Statements

Internal control evaluation as a nonaudit service

Paragraphs 3.97–3.98 of GAGAS	Requirements: Internal Control Evaluation as a Nonaudit Service
	3.97 Auditors should conclude that providing or supervising ongoing monitoring procedures over an entity's system of internal control impairs independence because the management participation threat created is so significant that no safeguards could reduce the threat to an acceptable level.
	3.98 Separate evaluations are sometimes provided as a nonaudit service. When providing separate evaluations as nonaudit services, auditors should evaluate the significance of the threat created by performing separate evaluations and apply safeguards when necessary to eliminate the threat or reduce it to an acceptable level.

When assessing whether separate evaluations of internal control create a threat to independence, items relevant to the assessment include the frequency of the separate evaluations as well as the scope or extent of the controls (in relation to the scope of the engagement conducted). Note that an internal control evaluation prepared as a nonaudit service is not a substitute for engagement procedures in a GAGAS audit.

Other nonaudit services that impair independence

Although some nonaudit services in the broad categories shown in the following paragraphs may not impair an auditor's independence, certain activities are specifically identified as impairing independence. As it relates to these activities performed as nonaudit services, there are no safeguards available that would eliminate a threat or reduce it to an acceptable level.

Paragraphs 3.96, 3.102, 3.104, & 3.106 of GAGAS	**Requirements: Internal Audit Assistance Provided by External Auditors**

Requirements: Internal Audit Assistance Provided by External Auditors

3.96 Internal audit assistance services involve assisting an entity in performing its internal audit activities. Auditors should conclude that the following internal audit assistance activities impair an external auditor's independence with respect to an audited entity:

a. setting internal audit policies or the strategic direction of internal audit activities;
b. performing procedures that form part of the internal control, such as reviewing and approving changes to employee data access privileges; and
c. determining the scope of the internal audit function and resulting work.

Requirements: Information Technology Services

3.102 Auditors should conclude that providing information technology (IT) services to an audited entity that relate to the period under audit impairs independence if those services include

a. designing or developing an audited entity's financial information system or other IT system that will play a significant role in the management of an area of operations that is or will be the subject matter of an engagement;
b. making other than insignificant modifications to source code underlying an audited entity's existing financial information system or other IT system that will play a significant role in the management of an area of operations that is or will be the subject matter of an engagement;
c. supervising audited entity personnel in the daily operation of an audited entity's information system; or
d. operating an audited entity's network, financial information system, or other IT system that will play a significant role in the management of an area of operations that is or will be the subject matter of an engagement.

Requirement: Appraisal, Valuation, and Actuarial Services

3.104 Auditors should conclude that independence is impaired if an audit organization provides appraisal, valuation, or actuarial services to an audited entity when (1) the services involve a significant degree of subjectivity and (2) the results of the service, individually or when combined with other valuation, appraisal, or actuarial services, are material to the audited entity's financial statements or other information on which the audit organization is reporting.

Requirement: Other Nonaudit Services

3.106 Auditors should conclude that providing certain other nonaudit services impairs an external auditor's independence with respect to an audited entity. These activities include the following:

a. Advisory service
   1. Assuming any management responsibilities
b. Benefit plan administration
   1. Making policy decisions on behalf of management
   2. Interpreting the provisions in a plan document for a plan participant on behalf of management without first obtaining management's concurrence
   3. Making disbursements on behalf of the plan
   4. Having custody of the plan's assets
   5. Serving in a fiduciary capacity, as defined under the Employee Retirement Income Security Act of 1974
c. Business risk consulting
   1. Making or approving business risk decisions
   2. Presenting business risk considerations to those charged with governance on behalf of management
d. Executive or employee recruiting
   1. Committing the audited entity to employee compensation or benefit arrangements
   2. Hiring or terminating the audited entity's employees
e. Investment advisory or management
   1. Making investment decisions on behalf of management or otherwise having discretionary authority over an audited entity's investments
   2. Executing a transaction to buy or sell an audited entity's investments
   3. Having custody of an audited entity's assets, such as taking temporary possession of securities

Internal auditors

Some entities employ auditors to work for entity management. These auditors may be subject to administrative direction from persons involved in the entity management process. Such audit organizations are internal audit functions and are encouraged to use the Institute of Internal Auditors' *International Standards for the Professional Practice of Internal Auditing*, in conjunction with GAGAS.

An internal audit organization may conduct engagements pertaining to external parties, such as contractors or entities subject to other outside agreements. If no impairments to independence exist, the audit organization can be considered independent as an external audit organization of those external parties.

Considerations regarding independence — Governments

The consideration of independence related to government audit organizations presents unique issues as discussed in this section. Because of constitutional or statutory requirements for which a government audit organization has no control over, the requirements in GAGAS may need to be modified. While the standards in chapter 3 of GAGAS apply to government audit organizations, independence requirements specifically related to government audit organizations are set forth in paragraph 3.84 of GAGAS. This guidance, as found earlier in this chapter, is related to reporting when an auditor in a governmental entity cannot apply safeguards to overcome an independence impairment but are required to perform the audit anyway. Some of the other considerations for government audit organizations follow here.

Engaging versus responsible party

In some cases, the engaging party who requests or requires an engagement differs from the party responsible for the engagement's subject matter. The GAGAS independence standards apply to the relationship between the auditors and the responsible party rather than the relationship between the auditors and the engaging party.

Examples of cases where the engaging party may differ from the responsible party include the following:

- A legislative body requires that auditors conduct, on the legislative body's behalf, a performance audit of program operations that are the responsibility of an executive agency. GAGAS requires that the auditors be independent of the executive agency.
- A state agency engages an independent public accountant to conduct an examination-level attestation engagement to assess the validity of certain information that a local government provided to the state agency. GAGAS requires that the independent public accountant be independent of the local government.
- A government department works with a government agency that conducts examination-level attestation engagements of contractor compliance with the terms and conditions of agreements between the department and the contractors. GAGAS requires that the auditors be independent of the contractors.

Structural threats for governmental audit organizations

Auditors in government may work under conditions that impair independence in accordance with GAGAS. An example of such a circumstance is a threat created by a statutory requirement for auditors to serve in official roles that conflict with the independence requirements of GAGAS, and for which there are no safeguards available to eliminate or reduce the threats to an acceptable level. This may happen if a law requires an auditor to serve as a voting member of an entity's management committee or board of directors. GAGAS provides standard language for modified GAGAS compliance statements for auditors who experience such impairments. Determining how to modify the GAGAS compliance statement in these circumstances is a matter of professional judgment.

The independence of an audit organization can be affected by its placement within a governmental entity and the structure of the government entity being audited. The structure can affect the audit organization's ability to perform work and report the results objectively.

Safeguards to mitigate structural threats to independence of audit organizations in government entities

The independence standard applies to auditors in both external audit organizations (reporting to third parties externally or to both internal and external parties) and internal audit organizations (reporting only to senior management within the audited entity). Such governmental audit organizations are often subject to constitutional or statutory safeguards that mitigate the effects of structural threats to independence.

For external audit organizations, constitutional or statutory safeguards that mitigate the effects of structural threats to independence may include governmental structures under which a government audit organization is

- at a level of government other than the one of which the audited entity is part (federal, state, or local) — for example, federal auditors auditing a state government program — or
- placed within a different branch of government from that of the audited entity — for example, legislative auditors auditing an executive branch program.

Safeguards other than those described previously may mitigate threats resulting from governmental structures. Structural threats may be mitigated for external audit organizations if the head of the audit organization meets any of the following criteria in accordance with constitutional or statutory requirements:

- Directly elected by voters of the jurisdiction being audited
- Elected or appointed by a legislative body, subject to removal by a legislative body, and reporting the results of engagements to and accountable to a legislative body
- Appointed by someone other than a legislative body, as long as the appointment is confirmed by a legislative body and removal from the position is subject to oversight or approval by a legislative body, and reports the results of engagements to and is accountable to a legislative body
- Appointed by, accountable to, reports to, and can be removed only by a statutorily created governing body, the majority of whose members are independently elected or appointed and are outside the organization being audited

GAGAS recognizes that there may be other organizational structures under which external audit organizations in government entities could be considered independent. If appropriately designed and implemented, these structures provide safeguards that prevent the audited entity from interfering with the audit organization's ability to perform the work and report the results impartially.

An external audit organization may be structurally independent under a structure different from ones discussed earlier in this section if the government audit organization is subject to all of the following constitutional or statutory provisions. These provisions may also be used as safeguards to augment those listed previously:

- Protections that prevent the audited entity from abolishing the audit organization
- Protections requiring that if the head of the audit organization is removed from office, the head of the agency reports this fact and the reasons for the removal to the legislative body
- Protections that prevent the audited entity from interfering with the initiation, scope, timing, and completion of any engagement
- Protections that prevent the audited entity from interfering with audit reporting, including the findings and conclusions or the manner, means, or timing of the audit organization's reports
- Protections that require the audit organization to report to a legislative body or other independent governing body on a recurring basis
- Protections that give the audit organization sole authority over the selection, retention, advancement, and dismissal of its personnel
- Access to records and documents related to the agency, program, or function being audited and access to government officials or other individuals as needed to conduct the engagement

If the head of the audit organization meets all of the following criteria, then government internal auditors who work under the direction of the audited entity's management are considered structurally independent for the purposes of reporting internally:

- Is accountable to the head or deputy head of the government entity or to those charged with governance
- Reports the engagement results both to the head or deputy head of the government entity and to those charged with governance
- Is located organizationally outside the staff or line management function of the unit under audit
- Has access to those charged with governance
- Is sufficiently removed from pressures to conduct engagements and report findings, opinions, and conclusions objectively without fear of reprisal

Other services provided by government audit organizations

Services provided by audit organizations in government entities frequently differ from the traditional professional services provided by an accounting or consulting firm to or for an audited entity. These types of services would generally not create a threat to independence as they are often provided in response to a statutory requirement, at the discretion of the authority of the audit organization, or to an engaging party (such as a legislative oversight body or an independent external organization) rather than a responsible party.

Examples of services provided by government audit organizations that would generally not create a threat to independence

- Providing information or data to a requesting party without auditor evaluation or verification of the information or data
- Developing standards, methodologies, audit guides, audit programs, or criteria for use throughout the government or for use in certain specified situations
- Collaborating with other professional organizations to advance auditing of government entities and programs
- Developing question and answer documents to promote understanding of technical issues or standards
- Providing assistance and technical expertise to legislative bodies or independent external organizations
- Assisting legislative bodies by developing questions for use at hearings
- Providing training, speeches, and technical presentations
- Providing assistance in reviewing budget submissions
- Contracting for audit services on behalf of an audited entity and overseeing the audit contract, as long as the overarching principles are not violated and the auditor under contract reports to the audit organization and not to management
- Providing audit, investigative, and oversight-related services that do not involve a GAGAS engagement, such as the following:
  - Investigations of alleged fraud, violation of contract provisions or grant agreements, or abuse
  - Periodic audit recommendation follow-up engagements and reports
  - Identifying best practices or leading practices for use in advancing the practices of government organizations

Documentation of independence considerations

Documentation of considerations regarding independence provides evidence of the auditor's judgments in forming conclusions regarding compliance with independence requirements. Specific requirements for documentation related to independence are found throughout chapter 3 of GAGAS, and as set forth in paragraph 3.107.

Paragraph 3.107 of GAGAS	Requirements: Documentation
	3.107 While insufficient documentation of an auditor's compliance with the independence standard does not impair independence, auditors should prepare appropriate documentation under the GAGAS quality control and assurance requirements. The independence standard includes the following documentation requirements, where applicable: a. document threats to independence that require the application of safeguards, along with safeguards applied, in accordance with the conceptual framework for independence as required by paragraph 3.33; b. document the safeguards in paragraphs 3.52 through 3.56 if an audit organization is structurally located within a government entity and is considered structurally independent based on those safeguards; c. document consideration of audited entity management's ability to effectively oversee a nonaudit service to be provided by the auditor as indicated in paragraph 3.74; d. document the auditor's understanding with an audited entity for which the auditor will provide a nonaudit service as indicated in paragraph 3.77; and e. document the evaluation of the significance of the threats created by providing any of the services discussed in paragraph 3.89.

Professional judgment

Paragraph 3.109 of GAGAS	Requirement: Professional Judgment
	3.109 Auditors must use professional judgment in planning and conducting the engagement and in reporting the results.

The following graph depicts the concept of professional judgment.

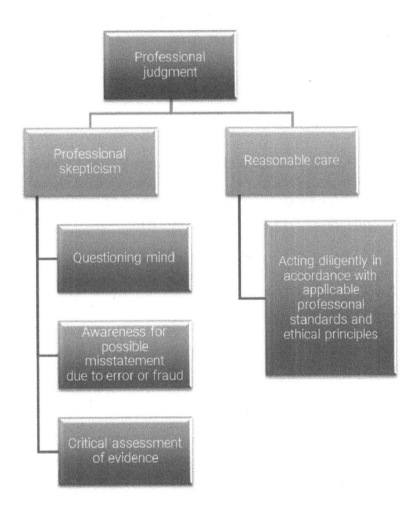

One of the cornerstones upon which GAGAS is based is the concept of professional judgment. Using professional judgment is important to auditors in carrying out all aspects of their professional responsibilities, including complying with the independence standards and the related conceptual framework. An auditor's professional responsibilities include maintaining objectivity and credibility; assigning competent personnel to the engagement; defining the scope of work; evaluating, documenting, and reporting the results of the work; and maintaining appropriate quality control over the engagement process.

The concept of professional judgment includes exercising reasonable care by acting diligently in accordance with applicable profession and ethical standards and exercising professional skepticism. In applying professional skepticism, evidence needs to be evaluated if it contradicts other evidence obtained or information that brings into question the reliability of documents or responses to inquiries to be used as evidence among other things. Further, it includes a mindset in which auditors assume that management is neither dishonest nor of unquestioned honesty. Auditors may accept records and documents as genuine unless they have reason to believe the contrary. Documentation of procedures undertaken to support such consideration may be appropriate when professional skepticism is applied in highly judgmental or subjective areas under audit.

A critical component of GAGAS engagements is using the auditor's professional knowledge, skills, and abilities, in good faith and with integrity, to diligently gather information and objectively evaluate the sufficiency and appropriateness of evidence.

> Professional judgment and competence are interrelated because judgments made depend upon the auditor's competence.

In addition to the professional judgment of individual auditors, professional judgment represents the application of the collective knowledge, skills, and abilities of all personnel involved with an engagement. Professional judgment may involve collaboration with other stakeholders, external specialists, and management in the audit organization as well as the auditors directly involved in the engagement.

With respect to applying the conceptual framework to determine independence in a given situation, the use of professional judgment is paramount. Professional judgment is needed when identifying and evaluating any threats to independence, including threats to the appearance of independence, and the related safeguards that may mitigate the identified threats.

Using professional judgment is also important to auditors in determining the necessary level of understanding of the engagement subject matter and related circumstances. Sound professional judgment is vital when considering whether the audit team's collective experience, training, knowledge, skills, abilities, and overall understanding are sufficient to gage the risks that the subject matter of the engagement may contain a significant inaccuracy or could be misinterpreted.

It is also important for an auditor to consider the risk level of each engagement, including the risk of arriving at improper conclusions. Within the context of audit risk, exercising professional judgment is integral to the engagement process when determining the sufficiency and appropriateness of evidence to be used to support the findings and conclusions based on the engagement objectives.

While the requirement to exercise professional judgment in planning and conducting an engagement places responsibility on each auditor and audit organization, it does not imply unlimited responsibility, nor does it imply infallibility on the part of either the individual auditor or the audit organization.

Absolute assurance is not attainable because of factors such as the nature of evidence and characteristics of fraud. Professional judgment does not mean eliminating all possible limitations or weaknesses associated with a specific engagement, but rather identifying, assessing, mitigating, and concluding on them.

Case study 3-2: Evaluation of nonaudit services

Audit Organization ABC is evaluating the different nonaudit services it provides to its various clients. Indicate whether the nonaudit service is any of the following:

- **Impairment** — Independence is impaired
- **Significant threat** — Evaluation of the threat is needed to determine if safeguards are available to eliminate the threat or reduce it to an acceptable level
- **Threat** — Evaluation of threat is needed to determine if the threat is a significant threat. If it is identified as a significant threat, the requirements related to significant threats apply
- **No threat** — Not considered a threat to independence

The first answer is given as an example.

Nonaudit service provided by Audit Organization ABC	Effect on independence
Hiring or terminating the audited entity's employees	Impairment
Preparing financial statements in their entirety from a client-provided trial balance	
Evaluation of an entity's system of internal control performed outside the audit	
Approving entity transactions	
Supervising ongoing monitoring procedures over an entity's system of internal control	
Preparing certain line items or sections of the financial statements based on information in the trial balance	
Preparing account reconciliations that identify reconciling items for the audited entity management's evaluation	
Changing journal entries without management approval	
Posting coded transactions to an audited entity's general ledger	
Educating the audited entity about matters that are readily available to the auditors, such as best practices or benchmarking studies	
Making changes to source documents without management's approval	

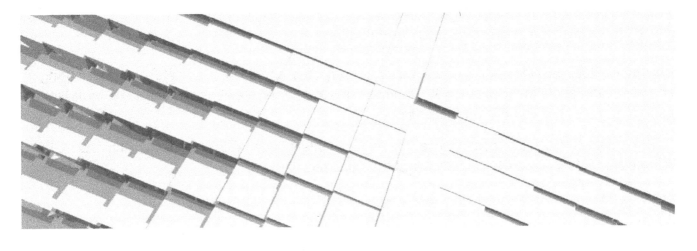

Chapter 4

Competence and Continuing Professional Education

Learning objectives

- Recognize the requirements related to competence found in generally accepted government auditing standards (GAGAS or the Yellow Book).

- Identify the indicators of competence when performing GAGAS audits.

- Identify the requirements related to continuing professional education (CPE).

- Recognize the types of programs and activities that qualify for GAGAS CPE.

Introduction

Chapter 4 establishes the GAGAS requirements for competence and CPE. Competence includes being knowledgeable about the specific GAGAS requirements and having the skills and abilities to proficiently apply that knowledge on GAGAS engagements.

CPE contributes to auditors' competence. The requirements included in this chapter are intended to be followed in conjunction with all other applicable GAGAS requirements.

Competence

GAGAS defines *competence* as the knowledge, skills, and abilities, obtained from education and experience, necessary to conduct the GAGAS engagement. Competence allows auditors to make sound professional judgments and includes possessing the technical knowledge, knowledge about GAGAS and skills necessary for the assigned role and the type of work being done.

Paragraphs 4.02–4.04 of GAGAS	Requirements: General
	4.02 The audit organization's management must assign auditors to conduct the engagement who before beginning work on the engagement collectively possess the competence needed to address the engagement objectives and perform their work in accordance with GAGAS.
	4.03 The audit organization's management must assign auditors who before beginning work on the engagement possess the competence needed for their assigned roles.
	4.04 The audit organization should have a process for recruitment, hiring, continuous development, assignment, and evaluation of personnel so that the workforce has the essential knowledge, skills, and abilities necessary to conduct the engagement. The nature, extent, and formality of the process will depend on various factors, such as the size of the audit organization, its structure, and its work.

Competence is achieved by a blending of education and experience. *Education* is defined as a structured and systematic process aimed at developing knowledge, skills, and other abilities that is often conducted in academic or learning environments. Experience refers to workplace activities that are relevant to developing professional proficiency. Years of auditing experience do not automatically result in competence, because such a quantitative measurement may not accurately reflect the kinds of experiences gained by auditors in any given time period. An important element for auditors is the maintenance of competence through a commitment to continued learning and development throughout their professional lives.

Indicators of competence

Certain technical knowledge, skills, and abilities are needed when conducting an engagement in accordance with GAGAS. These include the understanding necessary to proficiently apply the following:

- GAGAS
- Standards, statutory requirements, regulations, criteria, and guidance applicable to auditing or the objectives for the engagement(s) being conducted
- Techniques, tools, and guidance related to professional expertise applicable to the work being performed

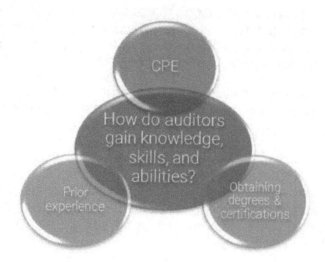

GAGAS notes that the audit organization and engagement teams may consider the levels of proficiency needed for each role on the engagement when assigning auditors to the engagement.

GAGAS defines the roles on the engagement to generally include the following:

Nonsupervisory auditors: Auditors in these roles plan or perform engagement procedures, requiring at least a basic level of proficiency. The work environment for these auditors has low levels of ambiguity, complexity, and uncertainty.

Supervisory auditors: Auditors in these roles plan engagements, perform engagement procedures, or direct engagements, requiring at least an intermediate level of competence. Work situations for these auditors involve moderate levels of ambiguity, complexity, and uncertainty.

Partners and directors: Auditors in these roles plan engagements, perform engagement procedures, or direct or report on engagements, requiring an advanced level of proficiency. Partners and directors may also be responsible for both reviewing engagement quality before issuing the report and for signing the report. The work environment for these auditors have high levels of ambiguity, complexity, and uncertainty.

In the context of the level of proficiency needed by roles on the audit, GAGAS provides the following definitions of key terms:

- **Planning:** Determining engagement objectives, scope, and methodology; establishing criteria to evaluate matters subject to audit; or coordinating the work of the other audit organizations. This definition excludes auditors whose role is limited to gathering information used in planning the engagement.
- **Directing:** Supervising the efforts of others who are involved in accomplishing the objectives of the engagement or reviewing engagement work to determine whether those objectives have been accomplished.
- **Performing engagement procedures:** Performing tests and procedures necessary to accomplish the engagement objectives in accordance with GAGAS.
- **Reporting:** Determining the report content and substance or reviewing reports to determine whether the engagement objectives have been accomplished and the evidence supports the report's technical content and substance before issuance. This includes signing the report.

Specialists

Paragraph 4.12 of GAGAS	Requirement: Specialists **4.12** The engagement team should determine that specialists assisting the engagement team on a GAGAS engagement are qualified and competent in their areas of specialization.

Some engagements necessitate the use of specialized techniques or methods that call for the skills of specialists. The GAGAS glossary defines *specialist* as an individual or organization possessing special skill or knowledge in a particular field other than accounting or auditing that assists auditors in conducting engagements. A specialist may be either an internal or external specialist.

> GAGAS does not consider individuals with special skills or knowledge related to specialized areas within the field of accounting or auditing, such as income taxation and information technology, to be specialists under this section. Such individuals are considered auditors.

Auditors rely on the competence and qualifications of specialists because those qualities significantly affect whether their work will be adequate for the engagement team's purposes and will meet GAGAS requirements. In the case of specialists, competence relates to the nature and level of expertise. The ability of specialists to exercise competence in the circumstances of the engagement despite any effects of bias, conflict of interest, or the influence of others may also be relevant in determining competence.

The following factors may assist the auditor in assessing the specialist's competence:

- The professional certification, license, or other recognition of the competence of the specialist in his or her field, as appropriate
- The professional and ethical reputation and standing of the specialist in the views of peers and others familiar with the specialist's capability or performance
- The specialist's experience and previous work in the subject matter
- The auditor's assessment of the specialist's knowledge and qualification based on previous experience using the specialist's work
- The specialist's knowledge of any technical performance standards or other professional or industry requirements in the specialist's field (for example, ethical standards and other membership requirements of a professional body or industry association, accreditation standards of a licensing body, or requirements imposed by law or regulation)
- The knowledge of the specialist with respect to relevant auditing standards
- The assessment of unexpected events, changes in conditions, or the evidence obtained from the results of engagement procedures that indicate it may be necessary to reconsider the initial evaluation of the competence and qualifications of a specialist as the engagement progresses

External specialists are not auditors subject to GAGAS CPE requirements. Internal specialists performing work in accordance with GAGAS as part of the engagement team — including planning, directing, and performing engagement procedures, or reporting on a GAGAS engagement — are considered auditors and are subject to GAGAS CPE requirements.

Knowledge check

1. GAGAS contains requirements and guidance related to competence for which of the following?

    a. Partners and directors, audited entity top level staff, and supervisory auditors.
    b. Nonsupervisory auditors, specialists, and partners and directors.
    c. Supervisory auditors, nonsupervisory auditors, and support staff.
    d. Supervisory auditors, nonsupervisory auditors, and audited entity finance office staff.

2. What auditor role is characterized by a work situation involving a high level of uncertainty, ambiguity and complexity and requires the highest level of proficiency when assigning auditors to an engagement?

    a. Those in a supervisory role.
    b. Those in a nonsupervisory role.
    c. Those participating as a specialist on the audit team.
    d. Partners and directors.

Continuing professional education

Government Auditing Standards – CPE alert

GAO issued an alert providing three exceptions and one clarification to an existing exemption to the *Government Auditing Standards* CPE requirements effective as of February 29, 2020. This alert applies to *Government Auditing Standards* CPE requirements only.

Exception: For 2-year CPE periods that end February 29, 2020 through December 31, 2020, auditors who have not completed the 80-hour or the 24-hour CPE requirements for the 2-year period may have up to 6 months immediately following the 2-year period to make up the deficiency. Any CPE hours completed toward a deficiency in one period may be documented in the CPE records and may not be counted toward the requirements for the next period.

Exception: Auditors are not required to complete at least 20 hours of CPE for a 1-year CPE period that ends February 29, 2020 through December 31, 2020.

Exception: From the audit organization's 2-year period in effect on February 29, 2020, auditors may carry over up to 40 hours of CPE, in excess of the 80-hour requirement, to the next CPE measurement period. For 2-year CPE measurement periods ending after December 31, 2020, only CPE hours earned through December 31, 2020 may be carried over. Auditors may not carry over excess CPE earned in prior 2-year CPE periods.

Clarification: For auditors who are not able to meet the *Government Auditing Standards* CPE requirements in *Government Auditing Standards* paragraphs 4.16 and 4.17, *Government Auditing Standards* paragraph 4.29 provides that the audit organization, at its discretion, may grant exemptions from a portion of the CPE requirement in the event of extended absences or other extenuating circumstances if specific situations prevent auditors from fulfilling those requirements and conducting engagements. If the auditor is working, including teleworking, audit organizations and auditors may not use this exemption. The exemption provided for under *Government Auditing Standards* paragraph 4.29 can only be used if the circumstances prevent the auditor from both fulfilling the CPE requirement and conducting *Government Auditing Standards* engagements. The audit organization may use its discretion to determine the portion of CPE hours from which the auditor is exempted. Audit organizations may consider prorating the requirement based on the number of full 6-month intervals remaining in the CPE period, as discussed in *Government Auditing Standards* paragraphs 4.42 and 4.43, but prorating using this calculation is not required.

Readers are encouraged to consult the full text of the alert at www.gao.gov/assets/710/706637.pdf.

Paragraph 4.16 of GAGAS	Requirements: General
	4.16 Auditors who plan, direct, perform engagement procedures for, or report on an engagement conducted in accordance with GAGAS should develop and maintain their professional competence by completing at least 80 hours of CPE in every 2-year period as follows.

CPE hours	Subject matter categories of CPE
24 hours	Subject matter directly related to the government environment, government auditing, or the specific or unique environment in which the audited entity operates
56 hours	Subject matter that directly enhance auditors' professional expertise to conduct engagements

4.17 Auditors should complete at least 20 hours of CPE in each year of the 2-year periods.

4.18 The audit organization should maintain documentation of each auditor's CPE.

GAGAS-specific CPE is recommended during years in which there are revisions to the standards to assist auditors in maintaining the competence necessary to conduct GAGAS engagements.

CPE used to fulfill the 24-hour requirement may be taken at any time during the 2-year measurement period.

Subject matter categories of CPE

Professional judgment is used by auditors and organization management when determining what subjects are appropriate for individual auditors in satisfying CPE requirements. Auditors may consider several factors when determining what specific subjects qualify for the CPE requirement including the types of knowledge, skills, and abilities, and the level of proficiency necessary to be competent for their assigned roles. Considering probable future engagements to which auditors may be assigned is also helpful when selecting specific CPE subjects to satisfy the 24-hour and the 56-hour CPE requirements. The audit organization is ultimately responsible for determining whether a subject or topic qualifies as acceptable for its auditors.

The subject matter categories for the 24-hour requirement are also permitted to be used to satisfy the 56-hour CPE requirement. If CPE in any of the subject matter and topics that would satisfy the 56-hour requirement is tailored specifically to the government environment, such CPE may qualify toward satisfying the 24-hour requirement. GAGAS provides a number of examples of CPE subjects that may qualify for each of the categories. Some of those examples follow.

24-hour requirement

Subject matter directly related to the government environment, government auditing, or the specific or unique environment in which the audited entity operates

- Generally accepted government auditing standards (GAGAS) and related topics, such as internal control as addressed in GAGAS
- The applicable American Institute of Certified Public Accountants' (AICPA) Statements on Auditing Standards
- U.S. generally accepted accounting principles, or the applicable financial reporting framework being used, such as those issued by the Federal Accounting Standards Advisory Board, the Governmental Accounting Standards Board, or the Financial Accounting Standards Board
- *Standards for Internal Control in the Federal Government* and *Internal Control — Integrated Framework*, as applicable
- Requirements for recipients of federal contracts or grants, such as single audits under the *Uniform Administrative Requirements, Cost Principles, and Audit Requirements for Federal Awards*
- Requirements for federal, state, or local program audits
- Fraud topics applicable to a government environment
- Statutory requirements, regulations, criteria, guidance, trends, risks, or topics relevant to the specific and unique environment in which the audited entity operates
- Performance auditing topics, such as obtaining evidence, professional skepticism, and other applicable audit skills
- Government ethics and independence
- Topics related to fraud, waste, abuse, or improper payments affecting government entities
- Compliance with laws and regulations
- Topics related to an internal specialist's area of knowledge

56-hour requirement

Subject matter that directly enhances auditors' professional expertise to conduct engagements

- Subject matter categories for the 24-hour requirement
- General ethics and independence
- Topics related to accounting, acquisitions management, asset management, budgeting, cash management, contracting, data analysis, program performance, or procurement
- Communicating clearly and effectively, both orally and in writing
- Managing time and resources
- Leadership
- Software applications used in conducting engagements
- Information technology
- Economics, human capital management, social and political sciences, and other academic disciplines that may be applied in engagements, as applicable.

Exemptions, exceptions, & prorations of the CPE requirements

When can an auditor be exempted from the GAGAS CPE requirements?

The audit organization has the ability to exempt certain individuals from the GAGAS CPE requirements when certain conditions are met. The audit organization may exempt auditors from the 56-hour CPE requirement, but not the 24-hour requirement, if they

- charge less than 20% of their time annually to engagements conducted in accordance with GAGAS and
- are only involved in performing engagement procedures, but not involved in planning, directing, or reporting on the engagement.

Provided that the audit organization has a basis for this determination and monitors actual time, the 20% may be based on historical or estimated charges in a year.

The audit organization may exempt nonsupervisory auditors from both the 24-hour and the 56-hour CPE requirements if they charge less than 40 hours of their time annually to GAGAS engagements. Furthermore, employees and contract employees that perform support services only are not considered auditors for GAGAS CPE purposes and therefore are not subject to the CPE requirements.

GAGAS also provides guidance regarding college and university students, who may be exempted from CPE requirement in certain situations, and auditors that have an extended absence due to a variety reasons, including maternity or paternity leave, extended family leave, sabbaticals, and military service.

> An audit organization may not grant exceptions for reasons such as workload, budget, or travel constraints.

When is it appropriate to prorate the GAGAS CPE requirements?

An auditor may prorate the number of required GAGAS CPE hours if they are hired or assigned to a GAGAS engagement after the beginning of an audit organization's two-year CPE period. GAGAS permits an audit organization to define a prorated number of hours based on the number of full six-month intervals remaining in the CPE period. For example, an audit organization that has a two-year CPE period running from January 1, 2021, through December 31, 2022, and that assigns a new auditor to a GAGAS engagement in May 2021, may calculate the prorated GAGAS CPE requirement for the auditor as follows:

- Number of full six-month intervals remaining in the CPE period: 3
- Number of six-month intervals in the full two-year period: 4
- Newly assigned auditor's GAGAS CPE requirement: 0.75×80 hours = 60 hours

Any proration of CPE hours related to the 24-hour requirement would be done in a similar way. The prorated number of hours would be the total requirement over the partial period, and the 20-hour minimum for each CPE year would not apply when the prorated number of hours is being used to cover a partial 2-year CPE period.

For auditors who change status such that they are charging more than 20% of their time annually to engagements under GAGAS, the audit organization may prorate the required CPE hours similar to when auditors are assigned to GAGAS engagements after the beginning of a two-year CPE measurement period.

> GAGAS CPE Deficiencies? At their discretion, GAGAS allows an audit organization to give auditors who have not completed the 80-hour CPE requirement for any 2-year period up to 2 months immediately following the 2-year period to make up the deficiency. They may also give auditors who have not completed the 20 hours of CPE in a 1-year period up to 2 months immediately following the 1-year period to make up the deficiency. However, any CPE hours completed toward a deficiency in one period may be documented in the CPE records and may not be counted toward the requirements for the next period. Audit organizations that grant the 2-month grace period may not allow auditors who have not satisfied the CPE requirements after the grace period to participate in GAGAS engagements until those requirements are satisfied.

What else do I need to know about CPE?

GAGAS does not permit the carryover of CPE hours earned in excess of the 80-hour and 24-hour requirements from one 2-year CPE measurement period to the next.

GAGAS does not require auditors to complete the CPE hours to satisfy the CPE requirements if an audit organization discontinues conducting GAGAS engagements or reassigns auditors to non-GAGAS assignments before auditors complete the CPE requirements. However, the audit organization may wish to have its auditors complete those requirements if it is foreseeable that the auditors will conduct GAGAS engagements in the future.

GAGAS provides two options to assist audit organizations to simplify the administration of the CPE requirements. An audit organization may establish a standard two-year period for all of its auditors, which can be on either 1) a fixed-year or 2) a rolling-year basis. A fixed-year measurement period, for example, would be the 2-year periods 2020 through 2021, 2022 through 2023, etc., and a rolling-year measurement period would be 2020 through 2021, 2021 through 2022, 2022 through 2023, and so forth.

An audit organization is permitted to use a measurement date other than the date it started its first GAGAS engagement, or it may choose to change its measurement date to coincide with a fiscal year or another reporting requirement, such as one established by a state licensing body or professional organization. For example, if an audit organization changes the end date of the measurement period from December 31 to June 30, during the audit organization's transition period (January 1 to June 30) its auditors may complete at least a prorated number of CPE hours for the 6-month transition period. The number of prorated hours required may be calculated using the method illustrated previously.

Programs and activities that qualify for CPE

CPE programs are structured educational activities or programs with learning objectives designed to maintain or enhance the auditors' competence to address engagement objectives and perform work in accordance with GAGAS.

Examples of structured educational programs and activities

- Internal training programs (e.g., courses, seminars, and workshops)
- Education and development programs presented at conferences, conventions, meetings, and seminars and meetings or workshops of professional organizations
- Training programs presented by other audit organizations, educational organizations, foundations, and associations
- Web-based seminars and individual study or eLearning programs
- Audio conferences
- Accredited university and college courses (credit and noncredit)
- Standard-setting organization, professional organization, or audit organization staff meetings when a structured educational program with learning objectives is presented (e.g., the portion of the meeting that is a structured educational program with learning objectives designed to maintain or enhance auditors' competence)
- Correspondence courses, individual study guides, and workbooks
- Serving as a speaker, panelist, instructor, or discussion leader at programs that qualify for CPE hours
- Developing or technical review of courses or the course materials for programs that qualify for CPE hours
- Publishing articles and books that contribute directly to the author's professional proficiency to conduct engagements

Examples of programs and activities that do **not** qualify for CPE hours under GAGAS

- On-the-job training
- Basic or elementary courses in subjects or topics in which auditors already have the knowledge and skills being taught
- Programs that are designed for general personal development, such as résumé writing, improving parent-child relations, personal investments and money management, and retirement planning
- Programs that demonstrate office equipment or software that is not used in conducting engagements
- Programs that provide training on the audit organization's administrative operations
- Business sessions at professional organization conferences, conventions, and meetings that do not have a structured educational program with learning objectives
- Conducting external quality control reviews
- Sitting for professional certification examinations

GAGAS CPE requirements may not be identical to state licensing requirements or requirements of professional organizations. Some subjects and topics may be acceptable for state licensing bodies or professional organizations but may not qualify as CPE under GAGAS. The reverse may also be true. Careful consideration of the requirements of relevant professional organizations and licensing bodies will assist in determining whether the CPE obtained meets the requirements of GAGAS and any other CPE requirements.

Training topics that may qualify as CPE for state licensing bodies or professional organizations but would not generally qualify as CPE for purposes of satisfying requirements under GAGAS include certain training in taxation, personal financial planning and investment, taxation strategies, estate planning, retirement planning, and practice management, unless such training directly enhances the auditors' professional proficiency to perform engagements or relate to the subject matter of an engagement. However, if certain taxation or other topics relate to an objective or the subject matter of an engagement, training in those related topics could qualify as CPE under GAGAS.

Though basic or elementary courses would generally not be acceptable for GAGAS CPE purposes, GAGAS states that they may be acceptable in cases where they are deemed necessary as "refresher" courses to enhance the auditors' proficiency to conduct audits and attestation engagements.

Although professional certification review courses may be counted toward the GAGAS CPE requirements, auditors may receive GAGAS CPE hours only for those segments of the review course that are relevant to the standards, statutory requirements, regulations, criteria, and guidance applicable to auditing or to the engagement objectives being performed, or for subject matter that directly enhances auditors' professional expertise to conduct engagements.

Knowledge check

3. Auditors performing work under GAGAS — including planning, directing, performing audit procedures, or reporting on an audit conducted in accordance with GAGAS — should maintain their professional competence through CPE. Which of the following is **not** a requirement under GAGAS?

   a. Auditors who plan engagement procedures for an engagement conducted in accordance with GAGAS should complete, in every 2-year period, at least 24 hours of CPE that directly relates to the government environment, government auditing, or the specific or unique environment in which the audited entity operates.
   b. Auditors who plan, direct, or report on an engagement conducted in accordance with GAGAS should obtain at least an additional 56 hours of CPE (for a total of 80 hours of CPE in every 2-year period) that enhances the auditor's professional expertise to conduct engagements.
   c. Auditors required to obtain 80 hours of CPE under the GAGAS requirements should complete at least 24 hours of CPE in each year of the 2-year period.
   d. Auditors hired or initially assigned to GAGAS audits after the beginning of an audit organization's 2-year CPE period may complete a prorated number of CPE hours.

How is GAGAS CPE measured?

One hour of CPE may be granted for each 50 minutes of participation in programs and activities that qualify.

Each unit of college credit under a semester system for university or college credit courses qualifies for 15 CPE hours, and each unit of college credit under a quarter system equals 10 CPE hours. CPE hours may be granted only for the actual classroom time for university or college noncredit courses.

CPE credit may be awarded if auditors complete the examination with a passing grade for individual study programs where successful completion is measured by a summary examination. Auditors in other individual study programs may obtain CPE hours when they satisfactorily complete the requirements of the self-study program. The number of hours granted may be based on the CPE provider's recommended number of CPE hours for the program.

To the extent that the subject matter contributes to auditors' competence, speakers, instructors, and discussion leaders at programs that qualify for CPE and auditors who develop or review the course materials qualify to receive CPE hours for preparation and presentation time. Guidelines for these hours are as follows:

- 1 CPE hour may be granted for each 50 minutes of presentation time.
- Up to 2 CPE hours may be granted for developing, writing, or advance preparation for each 50 minutes of the presentation.
- Auditors may not receive CPE hours for either preparation or presentation time for repeated presentations that they make within the 2-year period, unless the subject matter involved was changed significantly for each presentation.
- The maximum number of CPE hours that may be granted to an auditor as a speaker, instructor, discussion leader, or preparer of course materials may not exceed 40 hours for any 2-year period.

Articles, books, or materials written by auditors and published on subjects and topics that contribute directly to professional proficiency to conduct engagements qualify for CPE hours in the year they are published.

For each hour devoted to writing articles, books, or materials that are published, one CPE hour may be granted. However, CPE hours for published writings may not exceed 20 hours for any 2-year period.

Monitoring and documentation of CPE

GAGAS requires that the audit organization maintain documentation of each auditor's CPE. To assist in accomplishing this objective, GAGAS suggests that audit organization's policies and procedures for CPE include the following:

- Identify all auditors required to meet the CPE requirements.
- Provide auditors with the opportunity to attend internal CPE programs, external CPE programs, or both.
- Assist auditors in determining which programs, activities, and subjects qualify for CPE.

- Document the number of CPE hours completed by each auditor.
- Monitor auditor compliance with the CPE requirements to ensure that auditors complete sufficient CPE in qualifying programs and subjects.

Additionally, these policies and procedures for documentation should consider addressing the maintenance of documentation of the CPE hours completed by each auditor subject to the CPE requirements for an appropriate period of time to satisfy any legal and administrative requirements, including peer review. GAGAS permits the audit organization to either maintain documentation at the firm level or to delegate the responsibility to the individual auditor. However, if this responsibility is delegated, the audit organization should ensure adequate procedures are in place to ensure that its records of CPE hours earned by auditors are supported by the documentation maintained by auditors.

Sufficient evidence of completion of CPE may include a certificate or other evidence of completion if provided from the CPE provider for group and individual study programs. Other appropriate documentation of CPE completion includes copies of CPE courses presented or copies of course materials developed by or for speakers, instructors, or discussion leaders, along with a written statement supporting the number of CPE hours claimed; or a copy of the published book, article, or other material that name the writer as author or contributor, or a written statement from the writer supporting the number of CPE hours claimed.

GAGAS suggests that CPE compliance be monitored through an audit organization's internal inspections or other quality assurance monitoring activities. Although the audit organization is not required to prepare reports on CPE, the audit organization may consider preparing a periodic CPE report for distribution to the auditors or maintaining or accessing training data online to monitor its auditors' progress toward meeting the CPE requirements.

The suggested documentation to be maintained includes the following:

- The name of the organization providing the CPE
- The title of the training program, including the subject matter or field of study
- The dates attended for group programs or dates completed for individual study programs
- The number of CPE hours earned toward the 56-hour and 24-hour requirements
- Any reasons for specific exceptions granted to the CPE requirement
- Evidence of completion of CPE

Exercise 4-1 Yellow Book CPE

Draw a line to connect the CPE courses listed to the most likely CPE category under the Yellow Book. The first one has been done for you.

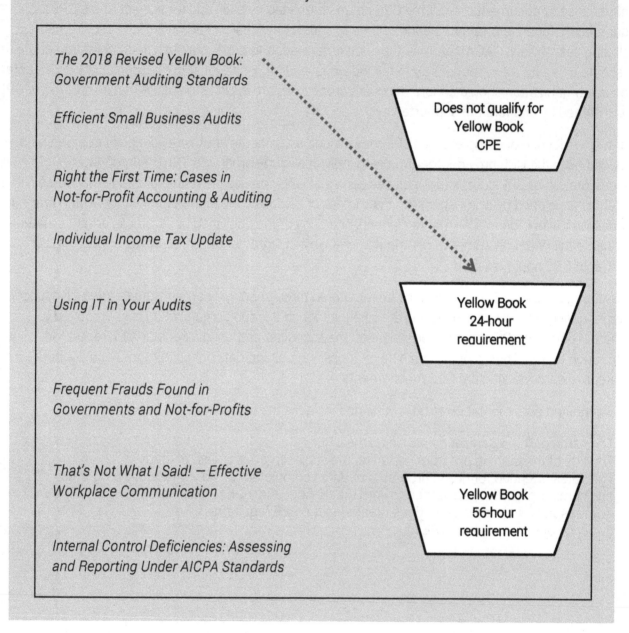

The 2018 Revised Yellow Book: Government Auditing Standards

Efficient Small Business Audits

Right the First Time: Cases in Not-for-Profit Accounting & Auditing

Individual Income Tax Update

Using IT in Your Audits

Frequent Frauds Found in Governments and Not-for-Profits

That's Not What I Said! — Effective Workplace Communication

Internal Control Deficiencies: Assessing and Reporting Under AICPA Standards

Does not qualify for Yellow Book CPE

Yellow Book 24-hour requirement

Yellow Book 56-hour requirement

Case study 4-1: DMV, CPAs, and the Yellow Book CPE requirements

DMV, CPAs is a local firm with 3 partners and 12 other staff. The firm's staff are used for audit, tax, and other client services. It is now early in 20X3 and Dan Dragster, CPA (audit partner) is sitting in his office pondering an upcoming peer review. Dan and one other partner (Brad Mustang) serve the firm's Yellow Book audit clients, which include several school district engagements and small not-for-profit entities. Dan and Brad have always been diligent in keeping up with their Yellow Book CPE, and relied on the manager who works on the Yellow Book audits (Bill Viper) to make sure that Bill and the other Yellow Book audit staff stay in compliance.

Dan has some concern over whether Bill has been keeping up with the staff's Yellow Book CPE for the latest two-year period (20X1 and 20X2). You are a manager who does not work on Yellow Book engagements, focusing instead on other areas of the practice. Dan approaches you and asks you to help by gathering the CPE hours of Bill and the other Yellow Book audit staff and try to determine whether they were in compliance.

Your first stop is at Bill's office, where he provides you with a spreadsheet that tracks the courses that Bill and the Yellow Book staff have taken in the last two years. You note that Bill has not filled in the columns that break out whether the courses taken qualify for the 24-hour component, the 56-hour component, or not at all toward the Yellow Book requirements.

Bill states that it is important for you to understand the following:

- Bill (as manager) and Irene Bentley (as senior) are involved in the planning, directing, performing field work, or reporting on the Yellow Book engagements.
- Sandy Dodge (audit staff) is involved only in performing audit procedures on the Yellow Book engagements. She spends approximately 30% of her time annually on the firm's Yellow Book engagements. Tom Sedan (staff assistant) is involved only in performing audit procedures on the Yellow Book engagements. He spends approximately 15% of his time annually on the firm's Yellow Book engagements.
- The firm's Yellow Book clients include several HUD and small not-for-profit entities, and Bill, Irene, Sandy, and Tom all work to some degree on each Yellow Book client.

Review the following spreadsheets listing the CPE courses taken by the staff and complete the columns breaking out whether the courses count toward the 24-hour component, the 56-hour component, or not at all toward the Yellow Book. Then conclude as to whether each staff member was in compliance with the Yellow Book requirements. Make your best attempt at this with the limited facts that you have (if you had more information than just the course titles, you could make more informed decisions).

Bill Viper, Manager					
Course title	Hours earned in 20X1	Hours earned in 20X2	Qualifies for the YB 24 hours	Qualifies for the YB 56 hours	Does not qualify for YB
Advanced Auditing of HHS Block Grants	8				
Individual Tax Update	8				
Financial and Tax Planning for High-Income Clients	8				
Recent Developments in Estate Planning	8				
The AICPA Guide to Consolidations, Business Combinations, and Combined Financial Statements	8				
Auditing Student Financial Aid		8			
Innovative Tax Planning for Individuals and Sole Proprietors		8			
Not-for-Profit Auditing: Auditing Financial Results		8			
Compilations and Reviews of Financial Statements		8			
Retirement Tax Planning that Works for Your Clients		8			
Total qualifying for the YB 24 hours Total qualifying for the YB 56 hours					
Did Bill meet the CPE requirements?					

Irene Bentley, Senior					
Course title	Hours earned in 20X1	Hours earned in 20X2	Qualifies for the YB 24 hours	Qualifies for the YB 56 hours	Does not qualify for YB
AICPA Form 990 Not-for-Profit Workshop[1]	8				
Not-for-Profit Auditing: Auditing Financial Results	8				
Becoming a 1040 Hero	8				
Recent Developments in Estate Planning	8				
Financial and Tax Planning for High-Income Clients	8				
Auditing Student Financial Aid		8			
Construction Contractors: Accounting and Auditing		8			
Not-for-Profit Accounting and Auditing Update Conference		16			
Forensic Auditing: Fraudulent Reporting and Concealed Assets		8			
Studies on Single Audit and Yellow Book Deficiencies		8			
Audits of Small Businesses		8			
Solving Complex Single Audit Issues for Government and Not-for-Profit Organizations		8			
Total qualifying for the YB 24 hours Total qualifying for the YB 56 hours					
Did Irene meet the CPE requirements?					

---

[1] Assume knowledge of the relevant tax requirements relates to an important financial reporting objective that influences reporting for purposes of the financial statements, such as categorization of expenses, prohibited transactions, or unrelated business taxable income.

Course title	Hours earned in 20X1	Hours earned in 20X2	Qualifies for the YB 24 hours	Qualifies for the YB 56 hours	Does not qualify for YB
Effective Internal Controls for Small Businesses	8				
Federal Tax Update for Individuals	8				
Cost Allocation Methods for Not-for-Profit Organizations	8				
Form 5500: Prepare it Fast – File it Right...The 1st Time[2]	8				
Reporting and Disclosure Problems for Small Businesses	8				
Using AICPA Audit and Accounting Guide Not-for-Profit Entities.	8				
Fraud and the Financial Statement Audit: Auditor Responsibilities Under AU-C section 240		8			
Innovative Tax Planning for Individuals		8			
Audit Staff Training: Level III		24			
Audits of Small Businesses		8			
Total qualifying for the YB 24 hours					
Total qualifying for the YB 56 hours					

Sandy Dodge, Staff

Did Sandy meet the CPE requirements?

---

[2] Assume the taxation or other topics in the course relate to an objective or subject matter of an audit engagement Sandy works on.

Course title	Hours earned in 20X1	Hours earned in 20X2	Qualifies for the YB 24 hours	Qualifies for the YB 56 hours	Does not qualify for YB
Tom Sedan, Staff Assistant					
Audits of Small Businesses	8				
Payroll Taxes and 1099s: Everything You Need to Know	16				
Employee Benefit Plans: Audit and Accounting Essentials	8				
Cash Flow Statement: Preparation, Presentation, and Use	8				
Audit Staff Training Level 1		24			
Federal Tax Update for Individuals		8			
Audits of Construction Contractors		8			

Total qualifying for the YB 24 hours
Total qualifying for the YB 56 hours

Did Tom meet the CPE requirements?

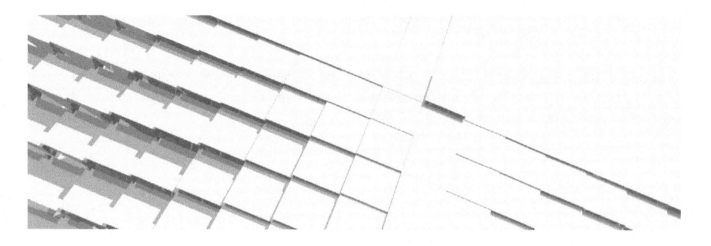

Chapter 5

Quality Control and Peer Review

Learning objectives

- Recognize the requirements related to establishing a system of quality control as found in generally accepted government auditing standards (GAGAS or the Yellow Book).

- Identify the GAGAS requirements for monitoring the system of quality control.

- Recognize the GAGAS requirements related to peer review.

Introduction

Chapter 5 of GAGAS establishes GAGAS requirements and guidance for quality control and assurance, and for administering, planning, performing, and reporting on peer reviews of audit organizations that conduct engagements in accordance with GAGAS.

Quality control and assurance

The 2018 Yellow Book emphasizes the topic of quality control and provides audit organizations with expanded guidance to assist them in implementing an effective program. An audit organization's system of quality control is one of the cornerstones of ensuring effective GAGAS engagements. GAGAS acknowledges that the nature, extent, and formality of an audit organization's quality control system will vary based on the audit organization's circumstances, such as size, number of offices and geographic dispersion, knowledge and experience of its personnel, nature and complexity of its engagement work, and cost-benefit considerations.

Paragraphs 5.02 & 5.04 of GAGAS	Requirements: Quality Control and Assurance
	5.02 An audit organization conducting engagements in accordance with GAGAS must establish and maintain a system of quality control that is designed to provide the audit organization with reasonable assurance that the organization and its personnel comply with professional standards and applicable legal and regulatory requirements.
	Requirement: System of Quality Control
	5.04 An audit organization should document its quality control policies and procedures and communicate those policies and procedures to its personnel. The audit organization should document compliance with its quality control policies and procedures and maintain such documentation for a period of time sufficient to enable those performing monitoring procedures and peer reviews to evaluate the extent to which the audit organization complies with its quality control policies and procedures.

The following graphic illustrates how the requirements set forth in chapter 5 of GAGAS, if properly implemented, form the cycle that will drive continuous improvement of an audit organization's system of quality control.

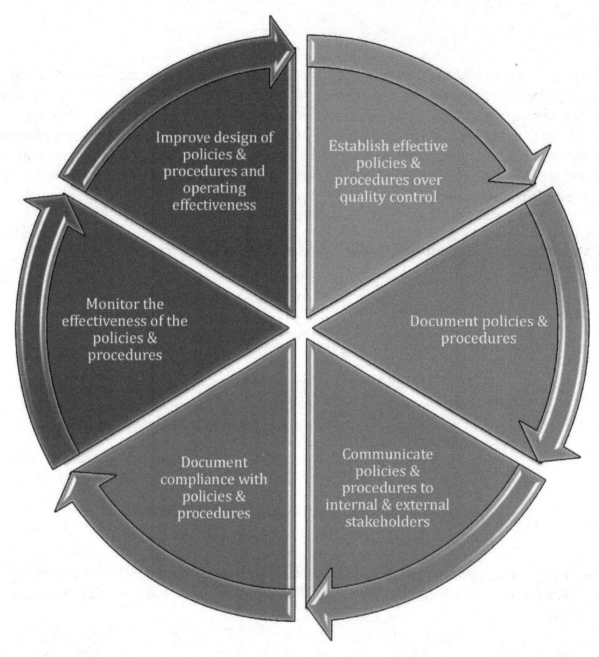

GAGAS has identified the following key components to be addressed by audit organizations when establishing and maintaining an effective system of quality control:

- Leadership responsibilities for quality within the audit organization
- Independence, legal, and ethical requirements
- Initiation, acceptance, and continuance of engagements
- Human resources
- Engagement performance including supervision
- Monitoring of quality

An audit organization's system of quality control is based on policies and procedures that address the key areas identified in GAGAS. The purpose of the policies and procedures is to provide reasonable assurance of complying with professional standards and applicable legal and regulatory requirements. Therefore, the design of the policies and procedures is an important factor in the system of quality control. The requirements and application guidance related to these areas will be explored in the following sections.

Leadership responsibilities for quality within the audit organization

Paragraphs 5.05–5.06 of GAGAS	Requirements: Leadership Responsibilities for Quality within the Audit Organization
	5.05 The audit organization should establish policies and procedures on leadership responsibilities for quality within the audit organization that include designating responsibility for quality of engagements conducted in accordance with GAGAS and communicating policies and procedures relating to quality.
	5.06 The audit organization should establish policies and procedures designed to provide reasonable assurance that those assigned operational responsibility for the audit organization's system of quality control have sufficient and appropriate experience and ability, and the necessary authority, to assume that responsibility.

Policies and communications in this area encourage a culture that recognizes that quality is essential in conducting GAGAS engagements, and that audit organization leadership is ultimately responsible for the system of quality control.

Independence, legal & ethical requirements

Paragraphs 5.08–5.09 of GAGAS	Requirements: Independence, Legal, and Ethical Requirements
	5.08 The audit organization should establish policies and procedures on independence and legal and ethical requirements that are designed to provide reasonable assurance that the organization and its personnel maintain independence and comply with applicable legal and ethical requirements.
	5.09 At least annually, the audit organization should obtain written affirmation of compliance with its policies and procedures on independence from all of its personnel required to be independent.

The development of policies and procedures related to independence and legal and ethical requirements help the audit organization to

- communicate its independence requirements to its personnel;
- identify and evaluate circumstances and relationships that create threats to independence; and
- take appropriate action to eliminate those threats or reduce them to an acceptable level by applying safeguards or, if considered appropriate, provide guidelines for withdrawing from an engagement where withdrawal is not prohibited by law or regulation.

The required written affirmation of compliance may be in paper or electronic form and if desired, an audit organization may obtain affirmations more frequently than once per year. For example, affirmations may be obtained on a per-engagement basis when such engagements last less than one year.

The benefit of obtaining written affirmation of retrospective compliance with the audit organization's policies and procedures on independence during a specified period is that the audit organization is able to demonstrate the importance that it attaches to independence to organization staff as well as keep the issue in the forefront of their minds by taking appropriate action on information indicating noncompliance, or potential noncompliance. Training personnel to always think and evaluate their independence assists the audit organization in complying with professional standards.

Initiation, acceptance, and continuance of engagements

Paragraph 5.12 of GAGAS	Requirement: Initiation, Acceptance, and Continuance of Engagements
	5.12 The audit organization should establish policies and procedures for the initiation, acceptance, and continuance of engagements that are designed to provide reasonable assurance that the organization will undertake engagements only if it *a.* complies with professional standards, applicable legal and regulatory requirements, and ethical principles; *b.* acts within its legal mandate or authority; and *c.* has the capabilities, including time and resources, to do so.

GAGAS recognizes that government audit organizations initiate engagements as a result of several factors, including legal mandates, requests from legislative bodies or oversight bodies, and audit organization discretion. When given a legal mandate or request, a government audit organization may be required to conduct the engagement, may not be permitted to make decisions about acceptance or continuance, and may not be permitted to resign or withdraw from the engagement. Consideration of these types of factors is needed when developing the policies and procedures of these audit organizations.

Audit organizations may consider their workloads when determining whether they have the resources to deliver the range of work to the desired level of quality. Audit organizations may operate with limited resources and may develop systems to prioritize their work in a way that accounts for the need to maintain quality.

Human resources

Paragraphs 5.15–5.16 of GAGAS	Requirements: Human Resources
	5.15 The audit organization should establish policies and procedures for human resources that are designed to provide the organization with reasonable assurance that it has personnel with the competence to conduct GAGAS engagements in accordance with professional standards and applicable legal and regulatory requirements.
	5.16 The audit organization should establish policies and procedures to provide reasonable assurance that auditors who are performing work in accordance with GAGAS meet the continuing professional education (CPE) requirements, including maintaining documentation of the CPE completed and any exemptions granted.

When considering the policies and procedures related to human resources, effective recruitment processes and procedures assist audit organizations in selecting individuals with the integrity and capabilities to develop the competence and skills necessary to perform the audit organization's work. In addition, effective performance evaluation, compensation, and advancement procedures give due recognition and reward to developing and maintaining competent personnel. In developing and maintaining competent personnel, an audit organization's policies and procedures may include the following steps:

- Communication of the audit organization's expectations regarding performance and ethical principles to personnel
- Providing personnel with effective evaluations of, and counseling on, performance, progress, and career development
- Communicating to personnel that compensation and advancement to positions of greater responsibility depend on, among other things, performance quality, and that consequences such as disciplinary action may occur for failure to comply with the audit organization's policies

GAGAS recognizes that both the size and circumstances of the audit organization affect the structure of the audit organization's performance evaluation process. Smaller audit organizations may employ less formal methods of evaluating the performance of its personnel. Furthermore, the audit organization may include contracting with external parties having suitable skills to conduct engagement work when internal resources are either unavailable or do not possess the necessary technical expertise. This factor may be included in policies and procedures.

Regardless of size, objectives of the audit organization's human resources policies and procedures may include

- promoting ongoing education and training for all personnel to encourage their professional development and to help ensure that personnel are up to date in current developments of the profession; and
- helping ensure that personnel and any parties contracted to carry out work for the audit organization have an appropriate understanding of the environment in which the organization operates and a good understanding of the work they are required to carry out.

Engagement performance

Paragraphs 5.22–5.25 of GAGAS	Requirements: Engagement Performance — General
	5.22 The audit organization should establish policies and procedures for engagement performance, documentation, and reporting that are designed to provide the audit organization with reasonable assurance that engagements are conducted and reports are issued in accordance with professional standards and applicable legal and regulatory requirements.
	5.23 If auditors change the engagement objectives during the engagement, they should document the revised engagement objectives and the reasons for the changes.
	5.24 The audit organization should establish policies and procedures designed to provide it with reasonable assurance that
	a. appropriate consultation takes place on difficult or contentious issues that arise among engagement team members in the course of conducting a GAGAS engagement;
	b. both the individual seeking consultation and the individual consulted document and agree upon the nature and scope of such consultations; and
	c. the conclusions resulting from consultations are documented, understood by both the individual seeking consultation and the individual consulted, and implemented.
	5.25 If an engagement is terminated before it is completed, and an audit report is not issued, auditors should document the results of the work to the date of termination and why the engagement was terminated.

Documentation

The audit organization's policies and procedures, as well as documentation of its compliance with those policies and procedures, may address a number of items, the form and content of which are matters of professional judgment and will vary based on circumstances of the organization. GAGAS permits documentation of policies and procedures and the organization' compliance with those policies and procedures to be either electronic or manual. Larger audit organizations may choose to use electronic databases to document matters such as independence confirmations, performance evaluations, and the results of monitoring while smaller audit organizations may decide that more informal documentation methods, such as manual notes, checklists, and forms, are more appropriate.

The audit organization's policies and procedures may take the form of written or electronic manuals, software tools, or other forms of standardized documentation, and industry-specific or subject matter-specific guidance materials, the purpose of which is to obtain consistency in the quality of engagement performance. Suggested topics to be addressed include the following:

- Maintaining current policies and procedures
- Standardizing conversations with the engagement team to provide an understanding of the engagement objectives and professional standards
- Complying with applicable engagement standards
- Planning the engagement, supervision, staff training, and mentoring
- Reviewing the work performed, the significant judgments made, and the type of report being issued
- Documenting the work performed, including and the timing and extent of review
- Reviewing the independence and qualifications of any specialists and the scope and quality of their work
- Resolving difficult or contentious issues or disagreements among team members, including specialists
- Obtaining and addressing comments from the audited entity on draft reports
- Reporting findings and conclusions supported by the evidence obtained and in accordance with professional standards and applicable legal and regulatory requirements

Engagement termination

Professional judgment is needed when determining whether and how to communicate the reason for terminating an engagement or changing the engagement objectives to those charged with governance, appropriate officials of the audited entity, the entity contracting for or requesting the engagement, and other appropriate officials as depends on the facts and circumstances.

Internal or external consultations

The GAGAS requirement regarding engagement performance contains a requirement that policies and procedures should be established and designed such that appropriate consultations takes place on difficult or contentious issues. GAGAS notes that consultation includes discussion at the appropriate professional level with individuals within or outside the audit organization who have relevant specialized expertise. Consultation includes the use of appropriate research resources, as well as the collective experience and technical expertise of the audit organization. GAGAS stresses the need for policies and procedures related to consultation as it helps promote quality and improves the application of professional judgment.

Recognition for the need of consultation in appropriate situations in the audit organization's policies and procedures helps promote a culture in which consultation is recognized as a strength, and personnel are encouraged to consult on difficult or contentious issues.

For effective consultation on significant technical, ethical, and other matters within or outside the audit organization, it is important that those consulted have the appropriate knowledge, authority, and experience, and be provided with all the relevant facts impacting the issue under consultation. It is essential that the conclusions from any consultations are both documented and implemented.

Documentation of consultations with other professionals that involve difficult or contentious matters is essential to the performance of the engagement as it contributes to an understanding of the issue on which consultation was sought and the results of the consultation, including any decisions made, the basis for those decisions, and how they were implemented.

An audit organization in need of externally provided specialized or technical consultation services can consider the use of other audit organizations, professional and regulatory bodies, and commercial organizations that provide relevant quality control services. Consideration of the external provider's competence and capabilities prior to contracting for the services assists in obtaining a qualified provider.

Supervision as part of engagement performance

Paragraphs 5.36–5.37 of GAGAS	Requirements: Engagement Performance — Supervision
	5.36 The audit organization should establish policies and procedures that require engagement team members with appropriate levels of skill and proficiency in auditing to supervise engagements and review work performed by other engagement team members.
	5.37 The audit organization should assign responsibility for each engagement to an engagement partner or director with authority designated by the audit organization to assume that responsibility and should establish policies and procedures requiring the organization to
	a. communicate the identity and role of the engagement partner or director to management and those charged with governance of the audited entity and
	b. clearly define the responsibilities of the engagement partner or director and communicate them to that individual.

Appropriate supervision of the audit team is an essential part of engagement performance. Suitable teamwork and training assist less experienced members of the engagement team to clearly understand the objectives of the assigned work and grow in their competency.

Suitable engagement supervision includes

- Tracking the progress of the engagement
- Evaluating the competence of individual members of the engagement team to ensure that they both understand their instructions and that the planned engagement approachis being followed
- Addressing significant findings and issues that arise during the engagement, considering their significance, and modifying the planned approach appropriately

---

- Identifying matters for consultation or consideration by engagement team members with appropriate levels of skill and proficiency in auditing, specialists, or both during the engagement

When reviewing the work performed by members of the audit team, a supervisor considers whether

- the work has been performed in accordance with professional standards and applicable legal and regulatory requirements;
- significant findings and issues have been appropriately raised for further consideration;
- appropriate consultations have occurred and the resulting conclusions are documented and implemented;
- the nature, timing, and extent of the work performed is appropriate without need for revision;
- the conclusions reached are appropriately supported by the work performed and is appropriately documented;
- the evidence obtained is sufficient and appropriate to support the report; and
- the objectives of the engagement procedures have been achieved.

GAGAS notes that, in the case of a sole proprietor, the requirement for a second auditor to review work performed and related documentation may be achieved through alternative procedures.

Knowledge check

1. Which of the following is required to be included in the quality control policies and procedures with respect to engagement performance?

    a. Policies and procedures related to personnel evaluations.
    b. Policies and procedures to ensure that the audit organization only undertakes engagements if it has the time and resources to do so.
    c. Policies and procedures on when and how to consult on complicated matters.
    d. Policies to ensure that those assigned responsibility for the system of quality control have the authority to assume that responsibility.

Monitoring of quality

GAGAS notes that monitoring of quality is a process that includes an ongoing consideration and evaluation of the audit organization's system of quality control including inspection of engagement documentation and reports for a selection of completed engagements. The objective of monitoring is to provide management of the audit organization with reasonable assurance that

- the policies and procedures related to the system of quality control are suitably designed and operating effectively in practice, and
- auditors have followed professional standards and applicable legal and regulatory requirements.

Paragraphs 5.42–5.46 of GAGAS	Requirements: Monitoring of Quality
	5.42 The audit organization should establish policies and procedures for monitoring its system of quality control.
	5.43 The audit organization should perform monitoring procedures that enable it to assess compliance with professional standards and quality control policies and procedures for GAGAS engagements. Individuals performing monitoring should have sufficient expertise and authority within the audit organization.
	5.44 The audit organization should analyze and summarize the results of its monitoring process at least annually, with identification of any systemic or repetitive issues needing improvement, along with recommendations for corrective action. The audit organization should communicate to the relevant engagement partner or director, and other appropriate personnel, any deficiencies noted during the monitoring process and recommend appropriate remedial action. This communication should be sufficient to enable the audit organization and appropriate personnel to take prompt corrective action related to deficiencies, when necessary, in accordance with their defined roles and responsibilities. Information communicated should include the following: *a.* a description of the monitoring procedures performed; *b.* the conclusions reached from the monitoring procedures; and *c.* when relevant, a description of systemic, repetitive, or other deficiencies and of the actions taken to resolve those deficiencies.
	5.45 The audit organization should evaluate the effects of deficiencies noted during monitoring of the audit organization's system of quality control to determine and implement appropriate actions to address the deficiencies. This evaluation should include assessments to determine if the deficiencies noted indicate that the audit organization's system of quality control is insufficient to provide it with reasonable assurance that it complies with professional standards and applicable legal and regulatory requirements, and that accordingly the reports that the audit organization issues are not appropriate in the circumstances.
	5.46 The audit organization should establish policies and procedures that require retention of engagement documentation for a period of time sufficient to permit those performing monitoring procedures and peer review of the organization to evaluate its compliance with its system of quality control or for a longer period if required by law or regulation.

The audit organization's unique facts and circumstances govern the monitoring procedures that should be applied. Monitoring is most effective when performed by individuals who do not have responsibility for the specific activity being monitored.

During the routine consideration and evaluation of the audit organization's system of quality control, issues may be identified that indicate changes are necessary to the audit organization's policies and procedures to provide the audit organization with reasonable assurance that its system of quality control is effective or to improve compliance.

Elements of ongoing consideration and evaluation procedures

- Review of selected administrative and human resource records pertaining to the quality control elements
- Review of engagement documentation and reports
- Discussions with the audit organization's personnel
- Determination of corrective actions to be taken and improvements to be made in the system, including providing feedback on the audit organization's policies and procedures relating to education and training
- Communication to appropriate audit organization personnel of weaknesses identified in the system, in the level of understanding of the system, or compliance with the system
- Follow-up by appropriate audit organization personnel so that necessary modifications are promptly made to the quality control policies and procedures

Monitoring assessments

- The appropriateness of the audit organization's guidance materials and any practice aids
- New developments in professional standards and applicable legal and regulatory requirements and how they are reflected in the audit organization's policies and procedures, when appropriate
- Written affirmation of compliance with policies and procedures on independence
- The effectiveness of staff training
- Decisions related to acceptance and continuance of relationships with audited entities and specific engagements
- Audit organization personnel's understanding of the organization's quality control policies and procedures and implementation thereof

GAGAS stresses that reviews of the work by engagement team members prior to the date of the report are not considered monitoring procedures and cannot be used to satisfy the monitoring requirements.

The extent of inspection procedures performed by an audit organization partially depends on the existence and effectiveness of the other monitoring procedures in place at the organization. GAGAS defines "inspection" as a retrospective evaluation of the adequacy of the audit organization's quality control policies and procedures, its personnel's understanding of those policies and procedures, and the extent of the audit organization's compliance with them. The nature of inspection procedures varies based on the audit organization's quality control policies and procedures and the effectiveness and results of other monitoring procedures and is subject to professional judgment.

Although the audit organization is required to analyze and summarize the results of its monitoring process at least annually, GAGAS permits the inspection of a selection of completed engagements to be performed on a cyclical basis to be determined by the audit organization. The organization of the inspection cycle and the timing of the selection of individual engagements depends on a number of factors, including the following:

- The size of the audit organization
- The number and geographical location of offices
- The results of previous monitoring procedures
- The degree of authority of both personnel and office (for example, whether individual offices are authorized to conduct their own inspections or whether only the head office may conduct them)
- The nature and complexity of the audit organization's practice and structure
- The risks associated with entities audited by the audit organization and with specific engagements

The audit organization has discretion in determining the scope of the individual engagements to be selected for inspection and may select engagements without prior notification to the engagement team. Selection of engagements may take into account the conclusions of a peer review or regulatory inspections.

The audit organization may summarize the inspection results when reporting identified deficiencies to individuals other than the relevant engagement partner or director. It is not necessary to identify the specific engagements concerned unless such identification is necessary for individuals other than the engagement partner or director to properly discharge their responsibilities.

Regardless of whether engagement documentation is in paper, electronic, or other form, the integrity, accessibility, and retrievability of the underlying information could be compromised if the documentation is altered, added to, or deleted without the auditors' knowledge or if the documentation is lost or damaged. This needs to be considered in order to protect the integrity of engagement documentation.

Examples of appropriate documentation relating to monitoring of the system of quality control include the following:

- Monitoring procedures, including the procedure for selecting completed engagements to be inspected
- A record of the evaluation of the following:
  - Adherence to professional standards and applicable legal and regulatory requirements
  - Whether the system of quality control was appropriately designed and is effectively implemented and operating
  - Whether the audit organization's quality control policies and procedures were appropriately applied so that the reports issued by the audit organization are appropriate in the circumstances
- Identification of the deficiencies noted, an evaluation of their effect, and the basis for determining whether and what further action is necessary

Knowledge check

2. All of the following items related to the results of an audit organization's monitoring process are required to be communicated to the relevant engagement partner or director, and other appropriate personnel **except**

    a. The date the monitoring procedures were performed.

    b. When relevant, a description of systemic, repetitive, or other deficiencies and of the actions taken to resolve those deficiencies.

    c. The conclusions reached from the monitoring procedures.

    d. A description of the monitoring procedures performed.

External peer review

The 2018 Yellow Book contains requirements and guidance for both audit organizations obtaining peer reviews and peer review teams performing peer reviews. The content that follows will mainly focus on the requirements and guidance for audit organizations obtaining peer reviews. However, some GAGAS requirements for peer review teams are included because that will assist audit organizations with managing their expectations in a peer review, both as it relates to the performance of the peer review and the reporting on it.

> The 2018 Yellow Book differentiates peer review requirements for audit organizations affiliated with one of five recognized organizations from those not affiliated with one of the recognized organizations. Audit organizations affiliated with one of the recognized organizations are required to comply with both the recognized organization's peer review requirements and those of GAGAS. Audit organizations not affiliated with a recognized organization are required to comply with GAGAS peer review requirements, some of which are specific to nonaffiliated audit organizations.

2018 Yellow Book — Peer review, audit organizations

Paragraphs 5.60–5.62 of GAGAS	**Requirement: General**
	5.60 Each audit organization conducting engagements in accordance with GAGAS must obtain an external peer review conducted by reviewers independent of the audit organization being reviewed. The peer review should be sufficient in scope to provide a reasonable basis for determining whether, for the period under review, (1) the reviewed audit organization's system of quality control was suitably designed and (2) the organization is complying with its quality control system so that it has reasonable assurance that it is performing and reporting in conformity with professional standards and applicable legal and regulatory requirements in all material respects.
	5.61 Audit organizations affiliated with one of the following recognized organizations should comply with the respective organization's peer review requirements and the requirements listed throughout paragraphs 5.66 through 5.80.
	a. American Institute of Certified Public Accountants
	b. Council of the Inspectors General on Integrity and Efficiency
	c. Association of Local Government Auditors
	d. International Organization of Supreme Audit Institutions
	e. National State Auditors Association
	5.62 Any audit organization not affiliated with an organization listed in paragraph 5.61 should meet the minimum GAGAS peer review requirements throughout paragraphs 5.66 through 5.94.

Audit organizations have discretion in selecting and accepting its peer review teams. Furthermore, GAGAS provides relief for audit organizations in cases of unusual difficulty or hardship. Extensions of the deadlines for submitting peer review reports exceeding 3 months beyond the due date may be granted by the entity that administers the peer review program with the concurrence of GAO.

Some audit organizations may be subject to or required to follow a peer review program of a recognized organization. However, some audit organizations may follow a specific peer review program voluntarily. In these voluntary instances, GAGAS requires audit organizations to comply with the recognized program's entire peer review process, including standards for administering, performing, and reporting on peer reviews, oversight procedures, training, and related guidance materials, where applicable.

Availability of the peer review report to the public

A peer review serves not only as a gage for audit organizations to assess the design and operational effectiveness of their system of quality control but also as a tool for the public and audited entities to make informed decisions when procuring high quality audit services. Public availability of GAGAS peer review reports assists with this.

Paragraphs 5.77–5.80 of GAGAS	Requirement: Availability of the Peer Review Report to the Public
	5.77 An external audit organization should make its most recent peer review report publicly available. If a separate communication detailing findings, conclusions, and recommendations is issued, the external audit organization is not required to make that communication publicly available. An internal audit organization that reports internally to management and those charged with governance should provide a copy of its peer review report to those charged with governance.
	5.78 An external audit organization should satisfy the publication requirement for its peer review report by posting the report on a publicly available website or to a publicly available file. Alternatively, if neither of these options is available, then the audit organization should use the same mechanism it uses to make other reports or documents public.
	5.79 Because information in peer review reports may be relevant to decisions on procuring audit services, an audit organization seeking to enter into a contract to conduct an engagement in accordance with GAGAS should provide the following to the party contracting for such services when requested: a. the audit organization's most recent peer review report and b. any subsequent peer review reports received during the period of the contract.
	5.80 Auditors who are using another audit organization's work should request a copy of that organization's most recent peer review report, and the organization should provide this document when it is requested.

To assist the public in understanding the peer review reports, an audit organization is permitted to include a description of the peer review process and how it applies to its organization. The following are some examples of additional information that audit organizations may provide to help users understand the meaning of the peer review report include the following:

- Explanation of the peer review process
- Description of the audit organization's system of quality control
- Explanation of the relationship of the peer review results to the audited organization's work
- If a peer review report is issued with a rating of pass with deficiencies or fail, explanation of the reviewed audit organization's plan for improving quality controls and the status of the improvements

Additional peer review requirements for audit organizations not affiliated with recognized organizations — Audit organizations

Paragraph 5.84 of GAGAS	Requirement: Peer Review Intervals
	5.84 An audit organization not already subject to a peer review requirement should obtain an external peer review at least once every 3 years. The audit organization should obtain its first peer review covering a review period ending no later than 3 years from the date an audit organization begins its first engagement in accordance with GAGAS.

Paragraph 5.86 of GAGAS	Requirement: Written Agreement for Peer Review
	5.86 The peer review team and the reviewed audit organization should incorporate their basic agreement on the peer review into a written agreement. The written agreement should be drafted by the peer review team, reviewed by the reviewed audit organization to ensure that it accurately describes the agreement between the parties, and signed by the authorized representatives of both the peer review team and the reviewed audit organization prior to the initiation of work under the agreement. The written agreement should state that the peer review will be conducted in accordance with GAGAS peer review requirements.

Generally, the period under peer review covers one year and a written agreement is required. The purpose of a written agreement is to ensure the agreement of both parties on the fundamental aspects of the peer review and to avoid any potential misunderstandings. GAGAS recommends that the written agreement address the following:

- Scope of the peer review
- Staffing and time frame

- Compensation for conducting the peer review, if applicable
- Preliminary findings, if applicable
- Reporting results
- Administrative matters
- Access to audit documentation

It is the responsibility of the peer review team to ensure that the peer review is conducted in accordance with GAGAS peer review requirements.

Peer review report response

When an audit organization receives a peer review rating of pass with deficiencies or fail that relates to its GAGAS engagements, critical evaluation of the design and implementation of the system of quality control is a factor in determining the audit organization's ability to accept and perform future GAGAS engagements.

Paragraphs 5.93–5.94 of GAGAS	Requirement: Audit Organization's Response to the Peer Review Report
	5.93 If the reviewed audit organization receives a report with a peer review rating of pass with deficiencies or fail, the reviewed audit organization should respond in writing to the deficiencies or significant deficiencies and related recommendations identified in the report.
	5.94 With respect to each deficiency or significant deficiency in the report, the reviewed audit organization should describe in its letter of response the corrective actions already taken, target dates for planned corrective actions, or both.

Paragraphs 5.75-.76 of GAGAS provide the following definitions for deficiencies and significant deficiencies as it relates to peer review reporting:

Deficiencies: Findings that because of their nature, causes, pattern, or pervasiveness, including their relative importance to the audit organization's system of quality control taken as a whole, could create a situation in which the audit organization would not have reasonable assurance of performing, reporting, or both in conformity with professional standards and applicable legal and regulatory requirements in one or more important respects.

Significant deficiencies: One or more deficiencies that the peer review team concludes result from a condition in the audit organization's system of quality control or compliance with that system such that the system taken as a whole does not provide reasonable assurance of performing, reporting, or both in conformity with professional standards and applicable legal and regulatory requirements.

The following exhibit provides information on the process of developing the reporting generated in a peer review by the peer reviewer.

Figure 3: Developing peer review communications for observed matters in accordance with generally accepted government auditing standards

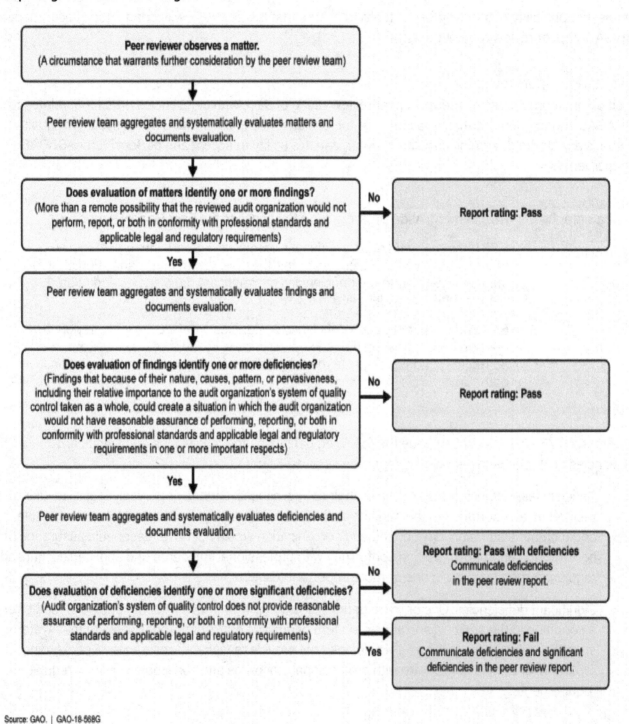

External peer review — Peer review teams

The information that follows is the Yellow Book guidance that relates primarily to peer review teams and includes the GAGAS requirements only.

2018 Yellow Book — Peer review, peer review teams

Paragraphs 5.66–5.67 of GAGAS	**Requirement: Assessment of Peer Review Risk** **5.66** The peer review team should perform an assessment of peer review risk to help determine the number and types of engagements to select for review. **5.67** Based on the risk assessment, the peer review team should select engagements that provide a reasonable cross section of all types of work subject to the reviewed audit organization's quality control system, including one or more engagements conducted in accordance with GAGAS.
Paragraphs 5.72–5.74 of GAGAS	**Requirement: Peer Review Report Ratings** **5.72** The peer review team should use professional judgment in deciding on the type of peer review rating to issue; the ratings are as follows a. Peer review rating of pass: A conclusion that the audit organization's system of quality control has been suitably designed and complied with to provide the audit organization with reasonable assurance of performing and reporting in conformity with professional standards and applicable legal and regulatory requirements in all material respects. b. Peer review rating of pass with deficiencies: A conclusion that the audit organization's system of quality control has been suitably designed and complied with to provide the audit organization with reasonable assurance of performing and reporting in conformity with professional standards and applicable legal and regulatory requirements in all material respects with the exception of a certain deficiency or deficiencies described in the report. c. Peer review rating of fail: A conclusion, based on the significant deficiencies described in the report, that the audit organization's system of quality control is not suitably designed to provide the audit organization with reasonable assurance of performing and reporting in conformity with professional standards and applicable legal and regulatory requirements in all material respects, or that the audit organization has not complied with its system of quality control to provide the audit organization with reasonable assurance of performing and reporting in conformity with professional standards and applicable legal and regulatory requirements in all material respects.

5.73 The peer review team should determine the type of peer review rating to issue based on the observed matters' importance to the audit organization's system of quality control as a whole and the nature, causes, patterns, and pervasiveness of those matters. The matters should be assessed both alone and in aggregate.

5.74 The peer review team should aggregate and systematically evaluate any observed matters (circumstances that warrant further consideration by the peer review team) and document its evaluation. The peer review team should perform its evaluation and issue report ratings as follows:

a. If the peer review team's evaluation of observed matters does not identify any findings (more than a remote possibility that the reviewed audit organization would not perform, report, or both in conformity with professional standards and applicable legal and regulatory requirements) or identifies findings that are not considered to be deficiencies, the peer review team issues a pass rating.

b. If the peer review team's evaluation of findings identified deficiencies but did not identify any significant deficiencies, the peer review team issues a pass with deficiencies rating and communicates the deficiencies in its report.

c. If the peer review team's evaluation of deficiencies identified significant deficiencies, the peer review team issues a fail rating and communicates the deficiencies and significant deficiencies in its report.

Additional peer review requirements for audit organizations not affiliated with recognized organizations — Peer review teams

Paragraph 5.82 of GAGAS	Requirement: Peer Review Scope
	5.82 The peer review team should include the following elements in the scope of the peer review:
	a. review of the audit organization's design of, and compliance with, quality control and related policies and procedures;
	b. consideration of the adequacy and results of the audit organization's internal monitoring procedures;
	c. review of selected audit reports and related documentation and, if applicable, documentation related to selected terminated engagements prepared in accordance with paragraph 5.25, if any terminated engagements are selected from the universe of engagements used for the peer review sample;
	d. review of prior peer review reports, if applicable;
	e. review of other documents necessary for assessing compliance with standards, for example, independence documentation, CPE records, and relevant human resource management files; and
	f. interviews with selected members of the audit organization's personnel in various roles to assess their understanding of and compliance with relevant quality control policies and procedures.

Paragraph 5.89 of GAGAS	Requirement: Peer Review Team
	5.89 The peer review team should meet the following criteria:
	a. The review team collectively has adequate professional competence and knowledge of GAGAS and government auditing.
	b. The organization conducting the peer review and individual review team members are independent (as defined in GAGAS) of the audit organization being reviewed, its personnel, and the engagements selected for the peer review.
	c. The review team collectively has sufficient knowledge to conduct a peer review.

Paragraph 5.91 of GAGAS	Requirement: Report Content
	5.91 The peer review team should prepare one or more written reports communicating the results of the peer review, which collectively include the following elements:
	a. a description of the scope of the peer review, including any limitations;
	b. a rating concluding on whether the system of quality control of the reviewed audit organization was adequately designed and complied with during the period reviewed and would provide the audit organization with reasonable assurance that it conformed to professional standards and applicable legal and regulatory requirements;
	c. specification of the professional standards and applicable legal and regulatory requirements to which the reviewed audit organization is being held;
	d. reference to a separate written communication, if issued under the peer review program;
	e. a statement that the peer review was conducted in accordance with GAGAS peer review requirements; and
	f. a detailed description of the findings, conclusions, and recommendations related to any deficiencies or significant deficiencies identified in the review.

Knowledge check

3. According to GAGAS requirements for audit organizations not affiliated with a recognized organization, an audit organization performing GAGAS audits should

    a. Obtain an external peer review at least once every two years.
    b. Obtain an external peer review after three years of performing GAGAS audits, then once every five years if there were no deficiencies found.
    c. Obtain an external peer review only if a client has requested a peer review report.
    d. Obtain an external peer review at least once every three years.

4. The peer review team uses professional judgment in deciding the type of peer review report to issue. Which of the following are types of peer review reports?

    a. Pass, fail, and fail with deficiencies.
    b. Pass, pass with deficiencies, and fail.
    c. Unmodified, qualified, adverse, and disclaimer.
    d. Pass or disclaimer.

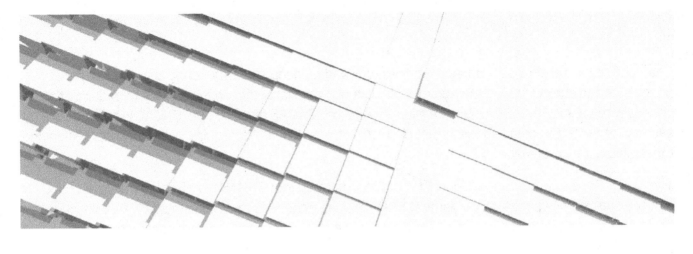

Chapter 6

Standards for Financial Audits

Learning objectives

- Recognize the relationship of generally accepted government auditing standards (GAGAS or the Yellow Book) and AICPA Statements on Auditing Standards (SASs).

- Identify the additional requirements for conducting financial audits in accordance with GAGAS.

- Recognize the concepts of waste and abuse.

- Identify the additional GAGAS requirements for reporting on financial audits.

Introduction

Chapter 6 of the Yellow Book contains requirements and guidance for conducting and reporting on financial audits subject to GAGAS. Auditors conducting financial audits under GAGAS are required to comply with the AICPA SASs, which are incorporated into GAGAS by reference. GAGAS incorporates all sections of the SASs, including the introduction, objectives, definitions, requirements, and application and other explanatory material.

The AICPA Code of Professional Conduct is not incorporated into GAGAS by reference; however, the GAO realizes that certified public accountants (CPAs) may use or be required to use the AICPA Code of Professional Conduct in conjunction with GAGAS in the performance of their engagements.

The guidance and requirements contained in chapters 1−5 of the Yellow Book also apply to financial audits under GAGAS.

Additional GAGAS requirements for conducting financial audits

Chapter 6 outlines additional requirements for conducting financial audits with respect to the following areas:

- Compliance with standards
- Licensing and certification
- Auditor communication
- Results of previous engagements
- Investigations or legal proceedings
- Noncompliance with provisions of laws, regulations, contracts, and grant agreements
- Findings
- Audit documentation
- Availability of individuals and documentation

Compliance with standards

Paragraph 6.02 of GAGAS	Requirement: Compliance with Standards
	6.02 GAGAS establishes requirements for financial audits in addition to the requirements in the AICPA SAS. Auditors should comply with these additional requirements, along with the AICPA requirements for financial audits, when citing GAGAS in financial audit reports.

The concept of materiality must be appropriately considered by auditors when planning and performing the audit using standards in conjunction with GAGAS. GAGAS engagements may warrant additional considerations by auditors. For instance, a lower materiality threshold may be appropriate for engagements conducted in accordance with GAGAS because of the public accountability of government entities and entities receiving government funding, various legal and regulatory requirements, and the visibility and sensitivity of government programs.

Licensing and certification

The 2018 revision of GAGAS expands the guidance related to licensing and certification of auditors, considering the global landscape in which professional services are provided.

Paragraphs 6.04–6.05 of GAGAS	Requirements: Licensing and Certification
	6.04 Auditors engaged to conduct financial audits in the United States who do not work for a government audit organization should be licensed CPAs, persons working for licensed certified public accounting firms, or licensed accountants in states that have multiclass licensing systems that recognize licensed accountants other than CPAs. **6.05** Auditors engaged to conduct financial audits of entities operating outside of the United States who do not work for a government audit organization should meet the qualifications indicated in paragraph 6.04, have certifications that meet all applicable national and international standards and serve in their respective countries as the functional equivalent of CPAs in the United States, or work for nongovernment audit organizations that are the functional equivalent of licensed certified public accounting firms in the United States.

Auditor communication

Paragraphs 6.06–6.07 of GAGAS	Requirements: Auditor Communication
	6.06 If the law or regulation requiring an audit specifically identifies the entities to be audited, auditors should communicate pertinent information that in the auditors' professional judgment needs to be communicated both to individuals contracting for or requesting the audit and to those legislative committees, if any, that have ongoing oversight responsibilities for the audited entity. **6.07** If the identity of those charged with governance is not clearly evident, auditors should document the process followed and conclusions reached in identifying the appropriate individuals to receive the required communications.

GAGAS stresses the importance of early communication to management or those charged with governance for some matters because of the relative significance and the urgency for corrective follow-up action. Furthermore, management benefits from early communication as it allows them to take prompt corrective action to prevent further occurrences when a control deficiency results in identified or suspected noncompliance with provisions of laws, regulations, contracts, and grant agreements or identified or suspected instances of fraud. When a deficiency is communicated early, GAGAS reporting requirements and application guidance is still applicable.

The governance structures of government entities and organizations can vary widely, and it may not always be clear as to who is charged with significant governance functions. In order to identify those charged with governance, an evaluation of the organizational structure is needed to determine the individuals directing and controlling operations, and how the audited entity delegates authority and establishes accountability for management. The process followed and the conclusion reached should be documented.

Paragraph 6.06 of GAGAS imposes a requirement in the event that a law or regulation that requires an audit specifically identifies the entities to be audited. To assist auditors in the determination of the applicability of this requirement, GAGAS provides an example of a law that does not specifically identify the entities to be audited. Though the Single Audit Act Amendments of 1996 outline the steps through which an auditee would be required to have a GAGAS audit, the law does not specifically identify the entities to be audited.

Evaluation of the results of previous engagements

GAGAS requires that auditors take steps to understand, evaluate, and use the results of previous engagements during the risk assessment process when planning an audit.

Paragraph 6.11 of GAGAS	Requirement: Results of Previous Engagements
	6.11 When planning the audit, auditors should ask management of the audited entity to identify previous audits, attestation engagements, and other studies that directly relate to the objectives of the audit, including whether related recommendations have been implemented. Auditors should evaluate whether the audited entity has taken appropriate corrective action to address findings and recommendations from previous engagements that could have a significant effect on the subject matter. Auditors should use this information in assessing risk and determining the nature, timing, and extent of current audit work and determining the extent to which testing the implementation of the corrective actions is applicable to the current audit objectives.

Investigations or legal proceedings

Paragraph 6.12 of GAGAS	Requirement: Investigations or Legal Proceedings
	6.12 Auditors should inquire of management of the audited entity whether any investigations or legal proceedings have been initiated or are in process with respect to the period under audit and should evaluate the effect of initiated or in-process investigations or legal proceedings on the current audit.

During the planning phase of the audit, GAGAS requires that auditors consider the presence of any investigations and legal proceedings to which the audited entity may be subject. Auditors may be required by laws, regulations, or policies to communicate indications of certain types of fraud or noncompliance with provisions of laws, regulations, contracts, and grant agreements to law enforcement or investigatory authorities before performing additional audit procedures.

It is important that auditors avoid interfering with investigations or legal proceedings when pursuing indicators of fraud and noncompliance with provisions of laws, regulations, contracts, and grant agreements. In certain circumstances, it may be suitable for the auditors to work with investigators or legal authorities or to withdraw from or defer further work on the engagement or a portion of the engagement to avoid hampering an ongoing investigation or legal proceeding.

Knowledge check

1. One of the additional requirements of GAGAS in a financial audit relates to previous audits and attestation engagements. What is the primary purpose of this additional requirement?

    a. To determine what issues arose in the prior audit so that the auditor can determine if they should accept the engagement.
    b. To determine if the auditor should issue an unmodified opinion on the financial statements.
    c. To be able to evaluate the honesty of audited entity officials.
    d. To be able to evaluate if the audited entity has taken appropriate corrective action to address significant findings and recommendations from the previous engagement.

2. As it relates to licensing and certifications, which statement is accurate when conducting a financial audit in accordance with GAGAS?

    a. All persons performing the engagement should be a licensed CPA, licensed accountant, or a person working for a licensed CPA firm.
    b. If working for a government audit organization, all persons performing the engagement should be a licensed CPA or licensed accountant.
    c. If engaged to conduct a GAGAS financial audit of an entity operating outside the United States, all persons performing the engagement must work for a U.S. licensed public accounting firm.
    d. If working for a government audit organization, meet the same requirements as those working for a CPA firm.

Noncompliance with provisions of laws, regulations, contracts, and grant agreements

Paragraph 6.15 of GAGAS	Requirement: Noncompliance with Provisions of Laws, Regulations, Contracts, and Grant Agreements
	6.15 Auditors should extend the AICPA requirements concerning consideration of noncompliance with laws and regulations to include consideration of noncompliance with provisions of contracts and grant agreements.

Government programs must comply with the provisions of many laws, regulations, contracts, and grant agreements—the significance of which varies widely based on the objectives of the audit. Accordingly, auditors may need additional information to help them determine the significance within the context of the audit objectives. Auditors may consider consulting with their legal counsel to

- determine those laws and regulations that are significant to the audit objectives,
- design tests of compliance with laws and regulations, and
- evaluate the results of those tests.

Consultation with legal counsel may also be appropriate when audit objectives require testing compliance with provisions of contracts or grant agreements. Auditors might consider consultation with others, such as investigative staff, other audit organizations or government entities that provided professional services to the audited entity, or applicable law enforcement authorities, to obtain information on compliance matters if the circumstances warrant such action.

Findings

Paragraphs 6.17–6.18 of GAGAS	Requirements: Findings
	6.17 When auditors identify findings, they should plan and perform procedures to develop the criteria, condition, cause, and effect of the findings to the extent that these elements are relevant and necessary to achieve the audit objectives.
	6.18 Auditors should consider internal control deficiencies in their evaluation of identified findings when developing the cause element of the identified findings.

Auditors may identify findings throughout the audit process that involve deficiencies in internal control; noncompliance with provisions of laws, regulations, contracts, and grant agreements; or instances of fraud. GAGAS provides guidance regarding the four elements of a finding in paragraphs 6.25–6.28, as set forth in the following exhibit.

Four elements of a finding

Criteria	Criteria include the laws, regulations, contracts, grant agreements, standards, measures, expected performance, defined business practices, and benchmarks against which performance is compared or evaluated. Criteria identify the required or desired state or expectation with respect to the program or operation. Criteria provide a context for evaluating evidence and understanding the findings, conclusions, and recommendations in the report. In a financial audit, the applicable financial reporting framework, such as generally accepted accounting principles, represents one set of criteria.
Condition	A condition is a situation that exists. The condition is determined and documented during the audit.
Cause	The cause is the factor or factors responsible for the difference between the condition and criteria. It may also serve as a basis for recommendations for corrective actions. Common factors include poorly designed policies, procedures, or criteria; inconsistent, incomplete, or incorrect implementation; or factors beyond the control of program management. Auditors may assess whether the evidence provides a reasonable and convincing argument for why the stated cause is the key factor contributing to the difference between the condition and the criteria.
Effect or potential effect	The effect or potential effect is the outcome or consequence resulting from the difference between the condition and the criteria. When the audit objectives include identifying the actual or potential consequences of a condition that varies (either positively or negatively) from the criteria identified in the audit, effect is a measure of those consequences. Effect or potential effect may be used to demonstrate the need for corrective action in response to identified problems or relevant risks.

When evaluating the underlying causes of findings, it is important to consider that, regardless of the type of finding identified, the cause of a finding may relate to one or more underlying internal control deficiencies. Depending on the magnitude of impact, likelihood of occurrence, and nature of the deficiency, the deficiency could be a significant deficiency or material weakness in a financial audit.

Often, considering internal control in the context of a comprehensive internal control framework can assist auditors in determining whether the root cause of an audit finding is from underlying internal control deficiencies. Identifying these deficiencies can help auditors develop meaningful recommendations for corrective action to management and those charged with governance. Frameworks such as GAO's *Standards for Internal Control in the Federal Government* (Green Book) or COSO's *Internal Control — Integrated Framework* provide suitable and available criteria against which management may evaluate and report on the effectiveness of the entity's internal control over financial reporting. Entities not required to use the Green Book, such as nonfederal entities, are permitted to adopt that guidance as a framework for an internal control system if desired.

Waste and abuse

Evaluating internal control in a government environment may also include considering internal control deficiencies that result in waste or abuse. Auditors are not required to perform specific procedures to detect waste or abuse in financial audits because GAGAS recognizes that the determination of waste and abuse is subjective. If, however, instances of waste or abuse are identified, auditors may consider whether and how to communicate such matters. Auditors may discover that waste or abuse are indicative of fraud or noncompliance with provisions of laws, regulations, contracts, and grant agreements.

Waste is the act of using or expending resources carelessly, extravagantly, or to no purpose. GAGAS states that waste can include activities that do not include abuse, and it does not necessarily involve a violation of law. Rather, waste relates primarily to mismanagement, inappropriate actions, and inadequate oversight.

Abuse is a behavior that is deficient or improper when compared with behavior that a prudent person would consider reasonable and necessary business practice given the facts and circumstances, but excludes fraud and noncompliance with provisions of laws, regulations, contracts, and grant agreements. Abuse includes misuse of authority or position for personal financial interests or those of an immediate or close family member or business associate.

Examples of waste

- Making travel choices that are contrary to existing travel policies or are unnecessarily extravagant or expensive
- Making procurement or vendor selections that are contrary to existing policies or are unnecessarily extravagant or expensive

Examples of abuse

- Creating unneeded overtime
- Requesting staff to perform personal errands or work tasks for a supervisor or manager
- Misusing the official's position for personal gain

Practice exercise

Exercise 6-1: Identifying elements of a finding

Directions

- Review the information in the right column in the following table regarding the audit of the City of Zahl.
- In the left column, write the basic element of a finding (criteria, condition, effect, or cause) to which the information in the right column relates. The first one has been done for you.

Cause	1. City officials explained that they were familiar with other grant programs where in-kind payments qualified as grant expenditures. They avowed not having read the fine print requirement for Urban Development Action Grant (UDAG) matching payments to be in cash and only for direct costs. The city officials who signed the grant said the matching requirement was not set forth in the documents they signed but acknowledged that it may have been in 20 or so pages of boilerplate attached to the documents.

	2. The city reported final project costs at $830,000 and city expenditures at $190,000. Review of the city records showed that, of the $190,000,
	
	   a. $110,000 was for land and rights-of-way the city already owned;
	   b. $60,200 was for all allocated salaries of city staff administering grant construction work that was done on contract; and
	   c. $19,800 was for meters and valves the city purchased for the project and provided to the contractor.

	3. The city is required by grant terms to expend $160,000 in matching payments on grant costs. Of the city's reported grant expenditures, only $19,800 qualifies as a matching payment. The difference of $140,200 qualifies as a liability, and this amount is considered material relative to the financial statements.
	4. The city of Zahl was awarded UDAG funding of $800,000 to extend its water and sewer system to a small industrial park. This improvement grant was awarded to attract a wholesale distribution firm that would develop the park and employ up to 100 people. Zahl is located at an intersection of three interstate highways.
	5. Recipients of UDAG funding are required by law to pay 20% of the amount of the awarded grant. This matching 20% must be in cash and expended on direct costs of the project.
	6. Zahl is a small city by UDAG criteria, and it meets UDAG criteria as a "distressed" area. The city lost 2 small manufacturing plants in the past year with a combined employment of 125 people.

Audit documentation

Because the AICPA SASs are incorporated by reference into GAGAS, auditors are required to follow the documentation guidance contained in generally accepted auditing standards (GAAS) as well as the additional documentation requirements of GAGAS.

Paragraphs 6.31–6.32 of GAGAS	Requirements: Audit Documentation
	6.31 Auditors should document supervisory review, before the report release date, of the evidence that supports the findings and conclusions contained in the audit report.
	6.32 Auditors should document any departures from the GAGAS requirements and the effect on the audit and on the auditors' conclusions when the audit is not in compliance with applicable GAGAS requirements because of law, regulation, scope limitations, restrictions on access to records, or other issues affecting the audit.

GAGAS clarifies that, when documenting departures from GAGAS, auditors should document departures both from unconditional and presumptively mandatory requirements when alternative procedures performed in the circumstances were not sufficient to achieve the objectives of the requirements.

Availablity of individuals and documentation

To maintain efficiency and avoid duplicative effort, GAGAS sets forth requirements that audit organizations in federal, state, and local governments and public accounting firms engaged to conduct financial audits in accordance with GAGAS cooperate in auditing programs of common interest so that auditors may use others' work. This may be facilitated by contractual arrangements that include provisions for full and timely access to appropriate individuals and to audit documentation.

Paragraph 6.34 of GAGAS	Requirement: Availability of Individuals and Documentation
	6.34 Subject to applicable provisions of laws and regulations, auditors should make appropriate individuals and audit documentation available upon request and in a timely manner to other auditors or reviewers.

Knowledge check

3. One of the elements of a finding is criteria. Which is **not** accurate regarding this element?

   a. This element provides a context for evaluating evidence and understanding the finding.
   b. Poorly designed policies and procedures may be one criterion.
   c. Expected performance may be one criterion.
   d. Laws and regulations may be one criterion.

4. Which is **not** an auditor consideration related to findings?

   a. Auditors should plan and perform procedures to develop the elements of a finding.
   b. Internal control deficiencies should be considered in the evaluation of identified finding when developing the cause element of a finding.
   c. Any instances of abuse that are identified during the audit must be reported as a finding.
   d. The effect of a finding includes potential effects resulting from the difference between the condition and the criteria.

Additional GAGAS requirements for reporting on financial audits

Chapter 6 of GAGAS outlines additional requirements for reporting on financial audits with respect to the following areas:

- Reporting the auditors' compliance with GAGAS
- Reporting on internal control; compliance with provisions of laws, regulations, contracts, and grant agreements; and instances of fraud
- Presenting findings in the audit report
- Reporting findings directly to parties outside the audited entity
- Obtaining and reporting the views of responsible officials
- Reporting confidential or sensitive information
- Distributing reports

Reporting on auditors' compliance with GAGAS

Paragraph 6.36 of GAGAS	Requirement: Reporting the Auditors' Compliance with GAGAS
	6.34 When auditors comply with all applicable GAGAS requirements, they should include a statement in the audit report that they conducted the audit in accordance with GAGAS.

GAGAS does not require auditors to cite compliance with the AICPA standards when citing compliance with GAGAS because the AICPA's financial audit standards are incorporated by reference. Also, GAGAS does not prohibit auditors from issuing a separate report conforming only to the requirements of the AICPA or other standards.

In the event that an auditor disclaims an opinion on a financial audit, the auditor may revise the GAGAS compliance statement. Determining how to revise the statement is a matter of professional judgment.

Reporting on internal control; compliance with provisions of laws, regulations, contracts, and grant agreements; and instances of fraud

Paragraphs 6.39–6.44 of GAGAS	Requirements: Reporting on Internal Control; Compliance with Provisions of Laws, Regulations, Contracts, and Grant Agreements; and Instances of Fraud
	6.39 Auditors should report on internal control and compliance with provisions of laws, regulations, contracts, or grant agreements regardless of whether they identify internal control deficiencies or instances of noncompliance.
	6.40 When providing an opinion or a disclaimer on financial statements, auditors should report as findings any significant deficiencies or material weaknesses in internal control over financial reporting that the auditors identified based on the engagement work performed.
	6.41 Auditors should include in their report on internal control or compliance the relevant information about noncompliance and fraud when auditors, based on sufficient, appropriate evidence, identify or suspect a. noncompliance with provisions of laws, regulations, contracts, or grant agreements that has a material effect on the financial statements or other financial data significant to the audit objectives or b. fraud that is material, either quantitatively or qualitatively, to the financial statements or other financial data significant to the audit objectives.
	6.42 Auditors should include either in the same or in separate report(s) a description of the scope of the auditors' testing of internal control over financial reporting and of compliance with provisions of laws, regulations, contracts, and grant agreements. Auditors should also state in the report(s) whether the tests they performed provided sufficient, appropriate evidence to support opinions on the effectiveness of internal control and on compliance with provisions of laws, regulations, contracts, and grant agreements.
	6.43 If auditors report separately (including separate reports bound in the same document) on internal control over financial reporting and on compliance with provisions of laws, regulations, contracts, and grant agreements, they should include a reference in the audit report on the financial statements to those additional reports. They should also state in the audit report that the reports on internal control over financial reporting and on compliance with provisions of laws, regulations, contracts, and grant agreements are an integral part of a GAGAS audit in considering the audited entity's internal control over financial reporting and compliance. If separate reports are used, the auditors should make the report on internal control and compliance available to users in the same manner as the financial audit report to which it relates.

6.44 Auditors should communicate in writing to audited entity officials when

a. identified or suspected noncompliance with provisions of laws, regulations, contracts, or grant agreements comes to the auditor's attention during the course of an audit that has an effect on the financial statements or other financial data significant to the audit objectives that is less than material but warrants the attention of those charged with governance or

b. the auditor has obtained evidence of identified or suspected instances of fraud that have an effect on the financial statements or other financial data significant to the audit objectives that are less than material but warrant the attention of those charged with governance.

GAGAS bases its requirement to report on internal control over financial reporting on the AICPA requirements to communicate significant deficiencies and material weaknesses in internal control over financial reporting identified during an audit in writing to those charged with governance.

The stated objective of the GAGAS internal control reporting requirement for financial audits is to increase the availability of information on significant deficiencies and material weaknesses to users of financial statements other than those charged with governance.

Internal control plays an expanded role in the government sector due to the government's accountability for public resources. It is significant because assessing internal control in a government environment may involve considering controls that would not be required in the private sector. Evaluating controls that are relevant to the audit encompasses understanding significant controls that the audited entity designed, implemented, and operated as part of its responsibility for oversight of public resources in the government sector.

Though comparative financial statements may be presented within a financial reporting package, the audit report on internal control and compliance with provisions of laws, regulations, contracts, and grant agreements relates only to the most recent reporting period included.

When identified or suspected noncompliance with provisions of laws, regulations, contracts, or grant agreements that does not warrant the attention of those charged with governance comes to the attention of the auditor, the determination of how to communicate such instances is a matter of professional judgment. However, if the matters identified are clearly inconsequential, professional judgment is needed when considering whether communication is necessary.

Auditors may consult with authorities or legal counsel about whether publicly reporting identified or suspected noncompliance with provisions of laws, regulations, contracts, or grant agreements or instances of fraud would compromise investigative or legal proceedings. Auditors are permitted to limit their public reporting to matters that would not hamper those proceedings, such as only reporting on information that is already a part of the public record.

Presenting findings in the audit report

Clearly developed findings help auditors make relevant recommendations for corrective action and assist management or oversight officials of the audited entity in understanding the need for corrective action. If auditors sufficiently develop the elements of a finding, they likely can provide more effective recommendations for corrective action.

Paragraphs 6.50–6.51 of GAGAS	Requirements: Presenting Findings in the Audit Report
	6.50 When presenting findings, auditors should develop the elements of the findings to the extent necessary to assist management or oversight officials of the audited entity in understanding the need for corrective action.
	6.51 Auditors should place their findings in perspective by describing the nature and extent of the issues being reported and the extent of the work performed that resulted in the finding. To give the reader a basis for judging the prevalence and consequences of these findings, auditors should, as appropriate, relate the instances identified to the population or the number of cases examined and quantify the results in terms of dollar value or other measures. If the results cannot be projected, auditors should limit their conclusions appropriately.

Reporting findings directly to parties outside the audited entity

GAGAS sets out certain circumstances in which it is appropriate for auditors to report directly to parties outside the audited entity. This is in addition to any legal requirements to report such information directly to parties outside the audited entity.

Paragraphs 6.53–6.55 of GAGAS	Requirements: Reporting Findings Directly to Parties Outside the Audited Entity
	6.53 Auditors should report identified or suspected noncompliance with provisions of laws, regulations, contracts, and grant agreements and instances of fraud directly to parties outside the audited entity in the following two circumstances.
	a. When audited entity management fails to satisfy legal or regulatory requirements to report such information to external parties specified in law or regulation, auditors should first communicate the failure to report such information to those charged with governance. If the audited entity still does not report this information to the specified external parties as soon as practicable after the auditors' communication with those charged with governance, then the auditors should report the information directly to the specified external parties.

Paragraphs 6.53–6.55 of GAGAS	**Requirements: Reporting Findings Directly to Parties Outside the Audited Entity (continued)**
	b. When audited entity management fails to take timely and appropriate steps to respond to fraud or noncompliance with provisions of laws, regulations, contracts, and grant agreements that (1) is likely to have a material effect on the subject matter and (2) involves funding received directly or indirectly from a government agency, auditors should first report management's failure to take timely and appropriate steps to those charged with governance. If the audited entity still does not take timely and appropriate steps as soon as practicable after the auditors' communication with those charged with governance, then the auditors should report the audited entity's failure to take timely and appropriate steps directly to the funding agency.
	6.54 Auditors should comply with the requirements in paragraph 6.53 even if they have resigned or been dismissed from the audit prior to its completion.
	6.55 Auditors should obtain sufficient, appropriate evidence, such as confirmation from outside parties, to corroborate representations by management of the audited entity that it has reported audit findings in accordance with provisions of laws, regulations, or funding agreements. When auditors are unable to do so, they should report such information directly as discussed in paragraphs 6.53 and 6.54.

Obtaining and reporting the views of responsible officials

Paragraphs 6.57–6.60 of GAGAS	**Requirements: Obtaining and Reporting the Views of Responsible Officials**
	6.57 Auditors should obtain and report the views of responsible officials of the audited entity concerning the findings, conclusions, and recommendations in the audit report, as well as any planned corrective actions.
	6.58 When auditors receive written comments from the responsible officials, they should include in their report a copy of the officials' written comments or a summary of the comments received. When the responsible officials provide oral comments only, auditors should prepare a summary of the oral comments, provide a copy of the summary to the responsible officials to verify that the comments are accurately represented, and include the summary in their report.
	6.59 When the audited entity's comments are inconsistent or in conflict with the findings, conclusions, or recommendations in the draft report, the auditors should evaluate the validity of the audited entity's comments. If the auditors disagree with the comments, they should explain in the report their reasons for disagreement. Conversely, the auditors should modify their report as necessary if they find the comments valid and supported by sufficient, appropriate evidence.

Paragraphs 6.57–6.60 of GAGAS	Requirements: Obtaining and Reporting the Views of Responsible Officials (continued)
	6.60 If the audited entity refuses to provide comments or is unable to provide comments within a reasonable period of time, the auditors should issue the report without receiving comments from the audited entity. In such cases, the auditors should indicate in the report that the audited entity did not provide comments.

GAGAS recommends providing a draft report with findings for review and comment by responsible officials of the audited entity and other relevant stakeholders to help the auditors develop a report that is fair, complete, and objective. Inclusion of the views of responsible officials within the report gives rise to a report that presents both the auditors' findings, conclusions, and recommendations as well as the perspectives of the audited entity's responsible officials and the corrective actions they plan to take.

It is preferable to obtain the comments in writing though oral comments are acceptable. When the audited entity provides technical comments in addition to the written or oral one, auditors may disclose in the report that technical comments were received. Technical comments address points of fact or are editorial in nature and do not address substantive issues, such as methodology, findings, conclusions, or recommendations.

Situations occur where obtaining oral comments may be appropriate. For instance, there may be times when a reporting date is critical to meeting a user's needs and the auditors have worked closely with the responsible officials throughout the engagement. In this case, the parties are familiar with the findings and issues addressed in the draft report. Another example is where the auditors do not expect major disagreements with findings, conclusions, or recommendations in the draft report or major controversies with regard to the issues discussed in the draft report.

Reporting confidential or sensitive information

Federal, state or local laws or regulations may prohibit public disclosure of classified or prohibited information. GAGAS acknowledges that there are sometimes situations where it is inappropriate to communicate information of a confidential or sensitive nature in a publicly available report. In such circumstances, auditors may issue a separate, classified, or limited use report containing the information and distribute the report only to persons authorized by law or regulation to receive it.

Circumstances involving public safety, privacy, or security concerns could also justify the exclusion of certain information from a publicly available or widely distributed report. GAGAS provides the example that detailed information related to computer security for a particular program may be excluded from publicly available reports because of the potential damage that misuse of this information could cause.

In these circumstances, auditors may issue a limited use report containing such information and distribute the report only to those parties responsible for acting on the auditors' recommendations. It may be appropriate to issue both a publicly available report with the sensitive information excluded and a limited use report in some cases. GAGAS recommends that auditors consult with legal counsel regarding any requirements or other circumstances that may necessitate omitting certain information. Consideration of the broad public interest in the program or activity under audit assists when deciding whether to exclude certain information from publicly available reports.

Paragraphs 6.63–6.65 of GAGAS	Requirements: Reporting Confidential or Sensitive Information
	6.63 If certain information is prohibited from public disclosure or is excluded from a report because of its confidential or sensitive nature, auditors should disclose in the report that certain information has been omitted and the circumstances that make the omission necessary.
	6.64 When circumstances call for omission of certain information from the report, auditors should evaluate whether this omission could distort the audit results or conceal improper or illegal practices and revise the report language as necessary to avoid report users drawing inappropriate conclusions from the information presented.
	6.65 When the audit organization is subject to public records laws, auditors should determine whether public records laws could affect the availability of classified or limited use reports and determine whether other means of communicating with management and those charged with governance would be more appropriate. Auditors use professional judgment to determine the appropriate means to communicate the omitted information to management and those charged with governance considering, among other things, whether public records laws could affect the availability of classified or limited use reports.

References to the omitted information within the report may be general and not specific and the report need not refer at all to its omission, if the omitted information is not necessary to meet the audit objectives.

Distributing reports

GAGAS sets forth the following requirements for distribution of reports issued for GAGAS audits.

Paragraph 6.70 of GAGAS	Requirement: Distributing Reports
	6.70 Distribution of reports completed in accordance with GAGAS depends on the auditors' relationship with the audited entity and the nature of the information contained in the reports. Auditors should document any limitation on report distribution.

Paragraph 6.70 of GAGAS	Requirement: Distributing Reports (continued)
	a. An audit organization in a government entity should distribute audit reports to those charged with governance, to the appropriate audited entity officials, and to the appropriate oversight bodies or organizations requiring or arranging for the audits. As appropriate, auditors should also distribute copies of the reports to other officials who have legal oversight authority or who may be responsible for acting on audit findings and recommendations and to others authorized to receive such reports.
	b. A public accounting firm contracted to conduct an audit in accordance with GAGAS should clarify report distribution responsibilities with the engaging party. If the contracting firm is responsible for the distribution, it should reach agreement with the party contracting for the audit about which officials or organizations will receive the report and the steps being taken to make the report available to the public.

Knowledge check

5. The requirements regarding presenting findings in the audit report includes all **except**

   a. Auditors should, as appropriate, relate instances of noncompliance identified to the population or number of cases examined and quantify the result of the testing.
   b. Auditors should describe the nature and extent of issues being reported.
   c. Auditors are required to provide recommendations for corrective action.
   d. Auditors should develop the elements of findings to the extent necessary to assist management and oversight officials in understanding the need for corrective action.

6. As it relates to reporting confidential or sensitive information, GAGAS guidance includes all **except**

   a. When auditors determine planned omitted material could distort the audit results or conceal improper or illegal practices, such information should not be omitted.
   b. If certain information is prohibited from public disclosure, auditors should disclose in the report that certain information has been omitted and the circumstances that make the omission necessary.
   c. Auditors may issue a separate, classified, or limited use report containing such information and distribute the report only to persons authorized by law or regulation to receive it.
   d. When circumstances call for omission of certain information, the reference to the omitted information may be general and not specific.

Case study

Case study 6-1: Drafting a finding

Directions

Review the following information from the audit of an entity:

- During our assessment of the entity's internal controls, we found that the entity was provided $100 million to carry out its programs. Program legislation and regulations imposed several requirements on the use of the funds. The entity has not established internal controls to ensure compliance with these requirements.
- Management of the entity is responsible for complying with laws and regulations. This responsibility includes establishing the necessary internal controls to ensure such compliance.
- Substantive audit tests for compliance with the requirements applicable to use of the funds did not reveal instances of noncompliance material to the financial statements. However, due to its significance, we consider this condition to be a material weakness in internal controls necessitating reporting. At the time of our audit the entity management had not undertaken the necessary steps to establish appropriate internal controls.
- The prior auditor found the same internal control problem during last year's audit.
- The entity's officials promised that they would establish and maintain internal controls that would help ensure compliance with appropriate laws and regulations.

Using the previous information, draft a finding using the following form. Also, complete the section regarding the auditor's recommendation, which is not required, but may be provided by the auditor. Although the auditor does not draft the management response, draft a response that management might provide to the auditor.

Criteria:	
Condition:	
Effect:	
Cause:	
Recommendation:	
Management Response:	

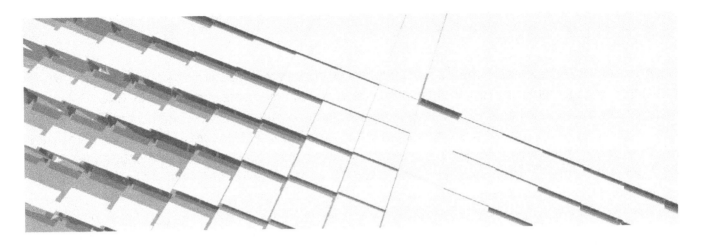

Chapter 7

Standards for Attestation Engagements and Reviews of Financial Statements

Learning objectives

- Identify the three types of attestation engagements found in generally accepted government auditing standards (GAGAS).

- Recognize the additional GAGAS requirements beyond those of the AICPA for attestation engagements.

- Recognize the additional GAGAS requirements beyond those of the AICPA for review of financial statement engagements.

Introduction

Chapter 7 of GAGAS addresses the requirements and guidance for performing and reporting on attestation engagements and review of financial statement engagements under GAGAS. GAGAS incorporates by reference AICPA's Statements on Standards for Attestation Engagements (SSAE) and AR-C section 90, *Review of Financial Statements* (AICPA, *Professional Standards*). All sections of the cited standards are incorporated, including the introduction, objectives, definitions, requirements, and application and other explanatory material. However, the AICPA Code of Professional Conduct is not incorporated by reference though GAGAS recognizes that certain CPAs may use or may be required to use the code in conjunction with GAGAS. Auditors should also comply with the guidance and requirements contained in chapters 1–5 of GAGAS when conducting attestation and review of financial statement engagements in accordance with GAGAS.

An attestation engagement can provide one of three levels of services defined by the AICPA, including

- examination engagements;
- review engagements; and
- agreed-upon procedures engagements.

GAGAS has outlined the additional standards beyond those required by the AICPA related to examination, review, agreed-upon procedures engagements, and review of financial statement engagements, organized by type of engagement, to help auditors quickly identify guidance applicable to the engagement they are performing. Not all of the additional standards are applicable to all types of engagements. However, for those applicable to a particular type of engagement, and after taking into account the varying levels of service, the supplementary standards are identical or nearly identical across types of engagements. Because of that similarity, the standards related to examination engagements are the focus of this chapter, with some application guidance provided for review engagements, agreed-upon procedures engagements, and review of financial statement engagements. The following chart demonstrates the supplementary standards beyond those required by the AICPA discussed in chapter 7 of GAGAS and the engagements to which they apply.

Additional standards	Examination	Review	Agreed-upon procedures	Review of financial statements
Compliance with standards	✓	✓	✓	✓
Licensing and certification	✓	✓	✓	✓
Auditor communication	✓			
Results of previous engagements	✓			
Investigations or legal proceedings	✓			

Additional standards	Examination	Review	Agreed-upon procedures	Review of financial statements
Noncompliance with provisions of laws, regulations, contracts, and grant agreements	✓	✓	✓	✓
Findings	✓			
Examination engagement documentation	✓			
Availability of individuals and documentation	✓			
Reporting the auditors' compliance with GAGAS	✓	✓	✓	✓
Reporting deficiencies in internal control	✓			
Reporting on noncompliance with provisions of laws, regulations, contracts, and grant agreements or instances of fraud	✓			
Presenting findings in the report	✓			
Reporting findings directly to parties outside the audited entity	✓			
Obtaining and reporting the views of responsible officials	✓			
Reporting confidential or sensitive information	✓			
Distributing reports	✓	✓	✓	✓

Establishing an understanding with the audited entity

The AICPA standards, which are used in conjunction with GAGAS, mandate that auditors establish an understanding with the audited entity with respect to the services to be performed for each attestation engagement or review of financial statement engagement. Establishing this understanding reduces the risk that either the auditors or the audited entity misinterpret the needs or expectations of the other party. The understanding includes the following:

- The objectives of the engagement
- Responsibilities of audited entity management
- Responsibilities of auditors
- Limitations of the engagement

Auditors often contract for GAGAS engagements with parties other than the officials of the audited entity, or as a result of a third-party request. Auditors in this situation may find it helpful to communicate information regarding the services to be performed to the individuals contracting for or requesting the engagement. Such an understanding may avoid any misunderstandings regarding the scope of the review or agreed-upon procedures engagement. For instance, a review engagement provides only limited assurance, and an agreed-upon procedures engagement does not provide an opinion or conclusion, and consequently, the work performed on both types of these GAGAS engagements by auditors is not sufficient to be able to develop elements of a finding or provide recommendations that are customary in other types of GAGAS engagements. As a result, requesting parties may find that a different type of attestation engagement or a performance audit may provide the appropriate level of assurance to meet their needs.

Examination engagements

Additional requirements beyond those of the AICPA for examination engagements

GAGAS establishes requirements for conducting and reporting on examination engagements in addition to the requirements contained in the AICPA standards. Nine of the additional standards involve conducting the GAGAS examination and the remaining eight standards relate to reporting. Auditors should comply with these additional requirements, along with the relevant AICPA standards for examination level attestation engagements, when citing GAGAS in their examination reports.

Compliance with standards

Paragraph 7.05 of GAGAS	Requirement: Compliance with Standards
	7.05 GAGAS establishes requirements for examination engagements in addition to the requirements for examinations contained in the AICPA SSAEs. Auditors should comply with these additional requirements, along with the AICPA requirements for examination engagements, when citing GAGAS in examination engagement reports.

Auditors are required by the AICPA standards applicable to examinations to properly apply the concept of materiality when planning and performing the audit. GAGAS engagements that concern government entities or entities that receive government awards may warrant additional considerations by auditors. For instance, a lower materiality threshold may be appropriate for engagements conducted in accordance with GAGAS because of the public accountability of government entities and entities receiving government funding, various legal and regulatory requirements, and the visibility and sensitivity of government programs.

Licensing and certification

The 2018 revision of GAGAS expands the guidance related to licensing and certification of auditors performing examination engagements, considering the global landscape in which professional services are provided.

Paragraphs 7.07–7.08 of GAGAS	Requirements: Licensing and Certification
	7.07 Auditors engaged to conduct examination engagements in the United States who do not work for a government audit organization should be licensed CPAs, persons working for licensed certified public accounting firms, or licensed accountants in states that have multiclass licensing systems that recognize licensed accountants other than CPAs.
	7.08 Auditors engaged to conduct examination engagements of entities operating outside of the United States who do not work for a government audit organization should meet the qualifications indicated in paragraph 7.07, have certifications that meet all applicable national and international standards and serve in their respective countries as the functional equivalent of CPAs in the United States, or work for nongovernment audit organizations that are the functional equivalent of licensed certified public accounting firms in the United States.

Auditor communication

Paragraphs 7.09–7.10 of GAGAS	Requirements: Auditor Communication
	7.09 If the law or regulation requiring an examination engagement specifically identifies the entities to be examined, auditors should communicate pertinent information that in the auditors' professional judgment needs to be communicated both to individuals contracting for or requesting the audit and to those legislative committees, if any, that have ongoing oversight responsibilities for the audited entity.
	7.10 If the identity of those charged with governance is not clearly evident, auditors should document the process followed and conclusions reached in identifying the appropriate individuals to receive the required communications.

GAGAS stresses the importance of early communication to management or those charged with governance for some matters identified in an examination engagement because of the relative significance and the urgency for corrective follow-up action. Additionally, early communication allows management to take prompt corrective action to prevent further occurrences when a control deficiency results in identified or suspected noncompliance with provisions of laws, regulations, contracts, and grant agreements or identified or suspected instances of fraud. When a deficiency is communicated early, GAGAS reporting requirements and application guidance related to examination engagements is still applicable.

The governance structures of government entities and organizations can vary, and it may not always be clearly evident who is charged with key governance functions. In order to identify those charged with governance an evaluation of the organizational structure is needed to determine the individuals directing and controlling operations, and how the audited entity delegates authority and establishes accountability for management. The auditors should document the process followed and the conclusion reached.

Evaluation of the results of previous engagements

GAGAS requires that auditors take steps to understand, evaluate, and use the results of previous engagements during the risk assessment process when planning an examination engagement.

Paragraph 7.13 of GAGAS	Requirement: Results of Previous Engagements
	7.13 When planning a GAGAS examination engagement, auditors should ask management of the audited entity to identify previous audits, attestation engagements, and other studies that directly relate to the subject matter or an assertion about the subject matter of the examination engagement, including whether related recommendations have been implemented. Auditors should evaluate whether the audited entity has taken appropriate corrective action to address findings and recommendations from previous engagements that could have a significant effect on the subject matter or an assertion about the subject matter. Auditors should use this information in assessing risk and determining the nature, timing, and extent of current work and determining the extent to which testing the implementation of the corrective actions is applicable to the current examination engagement objectives.

Investigations or legal proceedings

Paragraph 7.14 of GAGAS	Requirement: Investigations or Legal Proceedings
	7.14 Auditors should inquire of management of the audited entity whether any investigations or legal proceedings significant to the engagement objectives have been initiated or are in process with respect to the period under examination, and should evaluate the effect of initiated or in-process investigations or legal proceedings on the current examination engagement.

During the planning phase of the audit, GAGAS requires that auditors consider the presence of any investigations and legal proceedings to which the audited entity may be subject that relates to the subject matter of the examination. Auditors may be required by laws, regulations, or policies to communicate indications of certain types of fraud or noncompliance with provisions of laws, regulations, contracts, and grant agreements to law enforcement or investigatory authorities before performing additional examination procedures.

When auditors pursue indications of fraud and noncompliance with provisions of laws, regulations, contracts, and grant agreements, they should take care to avoid interference with investigations or legal proceedings. Auditors should consider whether it may be appropriate to work with investigators or legal authorities or to withdraw from or defer further work on the attestation engagement or a portion of the engagement to avoid interfering with an ongoing investigation or legal proceeding.

Noncompliance with provisions of laws, regulations, contracts, and grant agreements

Paragraph 7.17 of GAGAS	Requirement: Noncompliance with Provisions of Laws, Regulations, Contracts and Grant Agreements
	7.17 Auditors should extend the AICPA requirements concerning consideration of noncompliance with laws and regulations to include consideration of noncompliance with provisions of contracts and grant agreements.

GAGAS extends the provisions of AT-C section 205, *Examination Engagements*, (AICPA, *Professional Standards*) paragraphs .32 and .33 to noncompliance with provisions of contracts and grant agreements. Government programs are subject to provisions of numerous laws, regulations, contracts, and grant agreements. These provisions may vary in significance within the context of the engagement objectives and depends on the objectives of the specific engagement.

Auditors may find it helpful when navigating these provisions to consult with their legal counsel to

- determine those laws and regulations that are significant to the examination objectives,
- design tests of compliance with laws and regulations, and
- evaluate the results of those tests.

Consultation with legal counsel may also be appropriate when engagement objectives require testing compliance with provisions of contracts or grant agreements. Depending on the circumstances of the examination, auditors may consult with others, such as investigative staff, other audit organizations or government entities that provided professional services to the audited entity, or applicable law enforcement authorities, to obtain information on compliance matters.

Findings

Paragraphs 7.19–7.20 of GAGAS	Requirements: Findings
	7.19 When auditors identify findings, they should plan and perform procedures to develop the criteria, condition, cause, and effect of the findings to the extent that these elements are relevant and necessary to achieve the examination objectives.
	7.20 Auditors should consider internal control deficiencies in their evaluation of identified findings when developing the cause element of the identified findings.

Auditors may identify findings throughout the examination process that involve deficiencies in internal control; noncompliance with provisions of laws, regulations, contracts, and grant agreements; or instances of fraud.

In order for auditors to gain a full understanding of the findings and their repercussions, GAGAS instructs auditors performing examination engagements to plan and perform procedures to develop the criteria, condition, cause, and effect of the findings to the extent that these elements are relevant and necessary to achieve the examination objectives. The following chart describes each of the four elements of a finding, which mirror the definitions of the elements in a financial statement audit under GAGAS:

Four elements of a finding	
Criteria	Criteria include the laws, regulations, contracts, grant agreements, standards, measures, expected performance, defined business practices, and benchmarks against which performance is compared or evaluated. Criteria identify the required or desired state or expectation with respect to the program or operation. Criteria provide a context for evaluating evidence and understanding the findings, conclusions, and recommendations in the report.
Condition	A condition is a situation that exists. The condition is determined and documented during the attestation engagement.
Cause	The cause is the factor or factors responsible for the difference between the condition and the criteria and may also serve as a basis for recommendations for corrective actions. Common factors include poorly designed policies, procedures, or criteria; inconsistent, incomplete, or incorrect implementation; or factors beyond the control of program management. Auditors may assess whether the evidence provides a reasonable and convincing argument for why the stated cause is the key factor contributing to the difference between the condition and the criteria.

Four elements of a finding (continued)	
Effect or potential effect	The effect or potential effect is the outcome or consequence resulting from the difference between the condition and the criteria. When the engagement objectives include identifying the actual or potential consequences of a condition that varies (either positively or negatively) from the criteria identified in the engagement, effect is a measure of those consequences. Effect or potential effect may be used to demonstrate the need for corrective action in response to identified problems or relevant risks.

Regardless of the type of finding identified, when evaluating the underlying causes of findings it is important to consider that the cause of a finding may relate to one or more underlying internal control deficiencies. Depending on the magnitude of impact, likelihood of occurrence, and nature of the deficiency, the deficiency could be a significant deficiency or material weakness.

Considering internal control in the context of a comprehensive internal control framework can help auditors determine whether underlying internal control deficiencies exist as the root cause of findings. Identifying these deficiencies can help provide the basis for developing meaningful recommendations for corrective actions in an examination engagement under GAGAS. Frameworks such as GAO's *Standards for Internal Control in the Federal Government* (Green Book) or COSO's *Internal Control — Integrated Framework* provide suitable and available criteria against which management may evaluate and report on the effectiveness of the entity's internal control over financial reporting. Nonfederal entities are permitted to adopt the GAO's Green Book as a framework for an internal control system if desired.

Waste and abuse

Evaluating internal control in a government environment may also include considering internal control deficiencies that result in waste or abuse because of the concept of accountability for use of public resources and government authority. GAGAS recognizes that the determination of waste and abuse is subjective, and thus, auditors are not required to design and perform specific procedures to detect waste or abuse in examination engagements. However, if instances of waste or abuse are identified, auditors may consider whether and how to communicate such matters. Auditors may discover that waste or abuse are indicative of fraud or noncompliance with provisions of laws, regulations, contracts, and grant agreements.

Waste is the act of using or expending resources carelessly, extravagantly, or to no purpose. GAGAS states that waste can include activities that do not include abuse, and it does not necessarily involve a violation of law. Rather, waste relates primarily to mismanagement, inappropriate actions, and inadequate oversight. Examples of waste include:

- Making travel choices that are contrary to existing travel policies or are unnecessarily extravagant or expensive
- Making procurement or vendor selections that are contrary to existing policies or are unnecessarily extravagant or expensive

Abuse is defined as behavior that is deficient or improper when compared with behavior that a prudent person would consider reasonable and necessary business practice given the facts and circumstances. Abuse excludes fraud and noncompliance with provisions of laws, regulations, contracts, and grant agreements. Abuse includes misuse of authority or position for personal financial interests or those of an immediate or close family member or business associate. Examples of abuse include:

- Creating unneeded overtime
- Requesting staff to perform personal errands or work tasks for a supervisor or manager
- Misusing the official's position for personal gain

Examination engagement documentation

Because the AICPA SSAEs are incorporated by reference into GAGAS, auditors are required to follow the documentation guidance contained in AT-C section 205 paragraphs .87–.89 as well as additional relevant documentation requirements elsewhere within the attestation standards. However, GAGAS adds the following additional documentation requirements.

Paragraphs 7.33–7.34 of GAGAS	Requirement: Examination Engagement Documentation
	7.33 Auditors should comply with the following documentation requirements.
	a. Before the date of the examination report, document supervisory review of the evidence that supports the findings, conclusions, and recommendations contained in the examination report.
	b. Document any departures from the GAGAS requirements and the effect on the examination engagement and on the auditors' conclusions when the examination engagement does not comply with applicable GAGAS requirements because of law, regulation, scope limitations, restrictions on access to records, or other issues affecting the examination engagement.
	7.34 In addition to the requirements of the examination engagement standards used in conjunction with GAGAS, auditors should prepare attest documentation in sufficient detail to enable an experienced auditor, having no previous connection to the examination engagement, to understand from the documentation the nature, timing, extent, and results of procedures performed and the evidence obtained and its source and the conclusions reached, including evidence that supports the auditors' significant judgments and conclusions.

The examination engagement documentation requirements of GAGAS apply to departures from both unconditional and presumptively mandatory requirements when alternative procedures performed in the circumstances were not sufficient to achieve the objectives of the requirements when documenting departures from the GAGAS requirements.

The additional requirements of GAGAS related to documentation of examination engagements references an "experienced auditor." GAGAS defines an experienced auditor as an individual who possesses the competencies and skills to be able to conduct the examination engagement. These competencies and skills include an understanding of

- examination engagement processes and related examination standards,
- GAGAS and applicable legal and regulatory requirements,
- the subject matter on which the auditors are engaged to report,
- the suitability and availability of criteria, and
- issues related to the audited entity's environment.

Availablity of individuals and documentation

To maintain efficiency and avoid duplicative effort, GAGAS sets forth requirements that audit organizations in federal, state, and local governments and public accounting firms engaged to conduct GAGAS examination engagements in accordance with GAGAS cooperate in auditing programs of common interest so that auditors may use others' work. This may be, but is not required to be, facilitated by contractual arrangements that include provisions for full and timely access to appropriate individuals and to engagement documentation.

Paragraph 7.37 of GAGAS	Requirement: Availability of Individuals and Documentation
	7.37 Subject to applicable provisions of laws and regulations, auditors should make appropriate individuals and examination engagement documentation available upon request and in a timely manner to other auditors or reviewers.

Reporting on auditors' compliance with GAGAS

Paragraphs 7.39–7.40 of GAGAS	Requirements: Reporting the Auditors' Compliance with GAGAS
	7.39 When auditors comply with all applicable GAGAS requirements, they should include a statement in the report that they conducted the examination in accordance with GAGAS.
	7.40 If auditors report separately (including separate reports bound in the same document) on deficiencies in internal control; noncompliance with provisions of laws, regulations, contracts, and grant agreements; or instances of fraud, they should state in the examination report that they are issuing those additional reports. They should include a reference to the separate reports and also state that the reports are an integral part of a GAGAS examination engagement.

GAGAS does not require auditors to cite compliance with the AICPA standards when citing compliance with GAGAS. This is because GAGAS incorporates the AICPA's attestation standards by reference. Additionally, auditors are not prohibited from issuing a separate report conforming only to the requirements of the AICPA or other standards.

Reporting deficiencies in internal control

GAGAS outlines the following requirement when reporting on internal control deficiencies.

Paragraph 7.42 of GAGAS	Requirements: Reporting Deficiencies in Internal Control
	7.42 Auditors should include in the examination report all internal control deficiencies, even those communicated early, that are considered to be significant deficiencies or material weaknesses that the auditors identified based on the engagement work performed.

The auditor should exercise professional judgment when determining whether and how to communicate to officials of the audited entity internal control deficiencies that are not considered significant deficiencies or material weaknesses.

Reporting on noncompliance with provisions of laws, regulations, contracts, and grant agreements or instances of fraud in examination reports

Paragraphs 7.44–7.45 of GAGAS	Requirement: Reporting on Noncompliance with Provisions of Laws, Regulations, Contracts, and Grant Agreements or Instances of Fraud
	7.44 Auditors should include in their examination report the relevant information about noncompliance and fraud when auditors, based on sufficient, appropriate evidence, identify or suspect a. noncompliance with provisions of laws, regulations, contracts, or grant agreements that has a material effect on the subject matter or an assertion about the subject matter or b. fraud that is material, either quantitatively or qualitatively, to the subject matter or an assertion about the subject matter that is significant to the engagement objectives. **7.45** When auditors identify or suspect noncompliance with provisions of laws, regulations, contracts, or grant agreements or instances of fraud that have an effect on the subject matter or an assertion about the subject matter that are less than material but warrant the attention of those charged with governance, they should communicate in writing to audited entity officials.

Auditors are not required to, but are permitted to communicate to audited entity officials when auditors identify or suspect noncompliance with provisions of laws, regulations, contracts, or grant agreements or instances of fraud that do not warrant the attention of those charged with governance. This determination is a matter of professional judgment.

Auditors also are permitted to consult with authorities or legal counsel about whether publicly reporting identified or suspected noncompliance with provisions of laws, regulations, contracts, or grant agreements or instances of fraud would compromise investigative or legal proceedings. Auditors are allowed to limit their public reporting to matters that would not compromise those proceedings. For example, auditors may choose to only report on information that is already a part of the public record.

Presenting findings in the audit report

Although auditors are not required to provide recommendations for corrective action under GAGAS, clearly developed findings help auditors make relevant and effective recommendations for corrective action as well as assist management or oversight officials of the audited entity in understanding the need for corrective action. If auditors sufficiently develop the elements of a finding, they improve the relevance and effectiveness of any recommendations they make for corrective action.

Paragraphs 7.48–7.49 of GAGAS	Requirements: Presenting Findings in the Report
	7.48 When presenting findings, auditors should develop the elements of the findings to the extent necessary to assist management or oversight officials of the audited entity in understanding the need for corrective action.
	7.49 Auditors should place their findings in perspective by describing the nature and extent of the issues being reported and the extent of the work performed that resulted in the findings. To give the reader a basis for judging the prevalence and consequences of these findings, auditors should, as appropriate, relate the instances identified to the population or the number of cases examined and quantify the results in terms of dollar value or other measures. If the results cannot be projected, auditors should limit their conclusions appropriately.

Reporting findings directly to parties outside the audited entity

GAGAS sets out certain circumstances where it is appropriate for auditors to report directly to parties outside the audited entity. These reporting requirements are in addition to any legal requirements to report such information directly to parties outside the audited entity.

Paragraphs 7.51–7.53 of GAGAS	Requirements: Reporting Findings Directly to Parties Outside the Audited Entity
	7.51 Auditors should report identified or suspected noncompliance with provisions of laws, regulations, contracts, and grant agreements and instances of fraud directly to parties outside the audited entity in the following two circumstances.
	a. When audited entity management fails to satisfy legal or regulatory requirements to report such information to external parties specified in law or regulation, auditors should first communicate the failure to report such information to those charged with governance. If the audited entity still does not report this information to the specified external parties as soon as practicable after the auditors' communication with those charged with governance, then the auditors should report the information directly to the specified external parties.
	b. When audited entity management fails to take timely and appropriate steps to respond to fraud or noncompliance with provisions of laws, regulations, contracts, and grant agreements that is likely to have a material effect on the subject matter and involves funding received directly or indirectly from a government agency, auditors should first report management's failure to take timely and appropriate steps to those charged with governance. If the audited entity still does not take timely and appropriate steps as soon as practicable after the auditors' communication with those charged with governance, then the auditors should report the audited entity's failure to take timely and appropriate steps directly to the funding agency.
	7.52 Auditors should comply with the requirements in paragraph 7.51 even if they have resigned or been dismissed from the engagement prior to its completion.
	7.53 Auditors should obtain sufficient, appropriate evidence, such as confirmation from outside parties, to corroborate representations by management of the audited entity that it has reported audit findings in accordance with provisions of laws, regulations, or funding agreements. When auditors are unable to do so, they should report such information directly as discussed in paragraphs 7.51 and 7.52.

Obtaining and reporting the views of responsible officials

Paragraphs 7.55–7.58 of GAGAS	Requirements: Obtaining and Reporting the Views of Responsible Officials
	7.55 Auditors should obtain and report the views of responsible officials of the audited entity concerning the findings, conclusions, and recommendations in the examination report, as well as any planned corrective actions.
	7.56 When auditors receive written comments from the responsible officials, they should include in their report a copy of the officials' written comments or a summary of the comments received. When the responsible officials provide oral comments only, auditors should prepare a summary of the oral comments, provide a copy of the summary to the responsible officials to verify that the comments are accurately represented, and include the summary in their report.
	7.57 When the audited entity's comments are inconsistent or in conflict with the findings, conclusions, or recommendations in the draft report, the auditors should evaluate the validity of the audited entity's comments. If the auditors disagree with the comments, they should explain in the report their reasons for disagreement. Conversely, the auditors should modify their report as necessary if they find the comments valid and supported by sufficient, appropriate evidence.
	7.58 If the audited entity refuses to provide comments or is unable to provide comments within a reasonable period of time, the auditors should issue the report without receiving comments from the audited entity. In such cases, the auditors should indicate in the report that the audited entity did not provide comments.

GAGAS recommends that auditors provide a draft report with findings for review and comment by responsible officials of the audited entity and others to help the auditors develop a report that is fair, complete, and objective. A complete report includes both the auditors' findings, conclusions, and recommendations as well as the perspectives of the audited entity's responsible officials and the corrective actions they plan to take.

Though oral comments are permissible, best practices suggest that it is preferable to obtain the comments in writing. Auditors are permitted to disclose within the report that technical comments have been received in cases where the audited entity provided them in addition to their written or oral comments. Technical comments encompass points of fact or are editorial in nature and do not address substantive issues, such as methodology, findings, conclusions, or recommendations.

Some circumstances may warrant oral comments. For example, instances may occur where there is a reporting date critical to meeting a user's needs and auditors have worked closely with the responsible officials throughout the engagement and all parties have verbally agreed throughout the process with the findings. Furthermore, oral comments may be appropriate if the parties are familiar with the findings and issues addressed in the draft report or the auditors do not expect major disagreements with findings, conclusions, or recommendations in the draft report or major controversies with regard to the issues discussed in the draft report.

Reporting confidiential or sensitive information

Because of the unique nature of the public arena, there are sometimes situations where it is inappropriate for an auditor to communicate certain information of a confidential or sensitive nature in a publicly available report.

For example, federal, state or local laws or regulations may prohibit public disclosure of certain classified or otherwise prohibited information. In such circumstances, auditors are permitted under GAGAS to issue a separate, classified, or limited use report containing the information and distribute the report only to persons authorized by law or regulation to receive it.

Moreover, there may be circumstances involving public safety, privacy, or security concerns that could also justify the exclusion of certain information from a publicly available or widely distributed report. GAGAS provides the example that detailed information related to computer security for a particular program may be excluded from publicly available reports because of the potential damage that communication of the information could cause in the hands of the wrong user.

In these circumstances, auditors may issue a limited use report containing such information and distribute the report only to those parties responsible for acting on the auditors' recommendations. It may be appropriate to issue both a publicly available report with the sensitive information excluded and a limited use report. Consultation with legal counsel regarding any requirements or other circumstances that may necessitate omitting certain information is recommended. Consideration of the broad public interest in the program or activity under audit may assist when deciding whether to exclude certain information from publicly available reports.

Paragraphs 7.61–7.63 of GAGAS	Requirements: Reporting Confidential or Sensitive Information
	7.61 If certain information is prohibited from public disclosure or is excluded from a report because of its confidential or sensitive nature, auditors should disclose in the report that certain information has been omitted and the circumstances that make the omission necessary.
	7.62 When circumstances call for omission of certain information, auditors should evaluate whether this omission could distort the examination results or conceal improper or illegal practices and revise the report language as necessary to avoid report users drawing inappropriate conclusions from the information presented.

7.63 When the audit organization is subject to public records laws, auditors should determine whether public records laws could affect the availability of classified or limited use reports and determine whether other means of communicating with management and those charged with governance would be more appropriate. Auditors use professional judgment to determine the appropriate means to communicate the omitted information to management and those charged with governance considering, among other things, whether public records laws could affect the availability of classified or limited use reports.

References to the omitted information within the report are permitted to be general rather than specific in nature. In some instances, where the omitted information is not necessary to meet the engagement objectives, it may not be referenced at all.

As noted previously, GAGAS permits auditors to communicate general information in a written report and communicate detailed information orally in certain situations. The auditors may consult with legal counsel regarding applicable public records laws.

Distributing reports

GAGAS sets forth the following requirements for distribution of reports issued for examination engagements conducted in accordance with GAGAS.

Paragraph 7.69 of GAGAS	Requirement: Distributing Reports
	7.69 Distribution of reports completed in accordance with GAGAS depends on the auditors' relationship with the audited organization and the nature of the information contained in the reports. Auditors should document any limitation on report distribution.
	a. An audit organization in a government entity should distribute reports to those charged with governance, to the appropriate audited entity officials, and to the appropriate oversight bodies or organizations requiring or arranging for the examination engagements. As appropriate, auditors should also distribute copies of the reports to other officials who have legal oversight authority or who may be responsible for acting on audit findings and recommendations and to others authorized to receive such reports.
	b. A public accounting firm contracted to conduct an examination engagement in accordance with GAGAS should clarify report distribution responsibilities with the engaging party. If the contracting firm is responsible for the distribution, it should reach agreement with the party contracting for the examination engagement about which officials or organizations will receive the report and the steps being taken to make the report available to the public.

Knowledge check

1. Which of the following is accurate regarding the requirements for GAGAS attestation engagements?

   a. Auditors are required to comply only with GAGAS standards when citing GAGAS in their agreed-upon procedures report.
   b. Auditors are required to comply only with GAGAS standards when citing GAGAS in their review report.
   c. Auditors are required to comply only with AICPA standards when citing GAGAS in their agreed-upon procedures report.
   d. Auditors performing GAGAS attestation engagements should comply with both GAGAS and AICPA standards when citing GAGAS in their examination reports.

Attest review and agreed-upon procedures engagements

Additional requirements for review engagements beyond those of the AICPA

In addition to the requirements contained in the AICPA standards, GAGAS establishes requirements for performing and reporting on attest review and agreed-upon procedures engagements. Auditors should comply with these additional requirements, along with the relevant AICPA standards for review and agreed-upon procedures engagements, when citing GAGAS in their review and agreed-upon procedures reports. The requirements and guidance in chapters 1–5 and in chapter 7 of GAGAS apply. The additional GAGAS requirements for review engagements relate to the following areas:

- Compliance with standards
- Licensing and certification
- Noncompliance with provisions of laws, regulations, contracts, and grant agreements
- Reporting the auditors' compliance with GAGAS
- Distributing reports

GAGAS notes that when reporting the auditor's compliance with GAGAS for an attest review or an agreed-upon procedures engagement, it is important to include all the required reporting elements contained in the attestation standards incorporated by reference. Because review and agreed-upon procedures engagements are substantially less in scope than an audit or examination, including only the required or permitted reporting elements assists in ensuring that auditors comply with the standards and that users of the GAGAS review report understand the nature of the work performed and the results of the engagement.

The additional GAGAS requirements related to distributing reports issued for a review or agreed-upon procedures engagement include a requirement that report distribution be limited if the subject matter or the assertion that is the subject of the engagement involves material that is classified or contains confidential or sensitive information. Auditors should document any limitation on report distribution. This differs from the requirements under an examination as GAGAS does not provide for omitting sensitive or classified information from the reports.

Review of financial statement engagements

Additional requirements for a review of financial statements

GAGAS establishes requirements for performing and reporting on a review of financial statements in addition to the requirements for reviews of financial statements contained in the AICPA's AR-C section 90, *Review of Financial Statements*. Auditors should comply with these additional requirements, along with the relevant AICPA standards for a review of financial statements, when citing GAGAS in their reports. In addition to the requirements in chapters 1 through 5 of GAGAS, chapter 7 outlines additional requirements with respect to the following areas:

- Compliance with standards
- Licensing and certification
- Noncompliance with provisions of laws, regulations, contracts, and grant agreements
- Reporting the Auditors' Compliance with GAGAS
- Distributing reports

Because a review of financial statements is substantially less in scope than an audit or examination engagement, GAGAS stresses that it is important to include all required reporting elements contained in AR-C section 90, *Review of Financial Statements* used in conjunction with GAGAS. Including only those reporting elements required or permitted for a review of financial statements assists in ensuring that auditors comply with the standards and that users of the GAGAS report understand the nature of the work performed and the results of the engagement.

The additional GAGAS requirements for report distribution includes a requirement that report distribution be limited if the subject matter involves material that is classified or contains confidential or sensitive information. Auditors should document any limitation on report distribution. As with attest review and agreed-upon procedures engagements, this differs from the requirements under an examination as GAGAS does not provide for omitting sensitive or classified information from the reports.

Knowledge check

2. Which statement is accurate related to the additional GAGAS requirements for both attestation engagements and for review of financial statement engagements? Additional requirements related to

    a. Reporting deficiencies in internal control is applicable to all types of these engagements.
    b. Reporting the auditor's compliance with GAGAS is applicable only for the examination type of attestation engagement.
    c. Reporting findings directly to outside parties is not applicable to GAGAS agreed-upon procedures engagements.
    d. The requirements related to findings is applicable to a review of financial statement engagement.

3. Which of the following is accurate regarding the additional GAGAS requirements for engagements related to an agreed-upon procedures engagement?

    a. Persons engaged to conduct an agreed-upon procedures engagement outside of the United States who do not work for a government audit organization must work for a U.S. licensed certified public accounting firm.

    b. Auditors are required to include all the required reporting elements related to agreed-upon procedures contained in the SSAEs when citing GAGAS in their agreed-upon procedures reports.

    c. AICPA requirements concerning the consideration of noncompliance with laws and regulations should not be extended to also include noncompliance with provisions of contracts and grant agreements.

    d. When auditors identify findings, they should plan and perform procedures to develop the criteria, condition, cause, and effect of the findings.

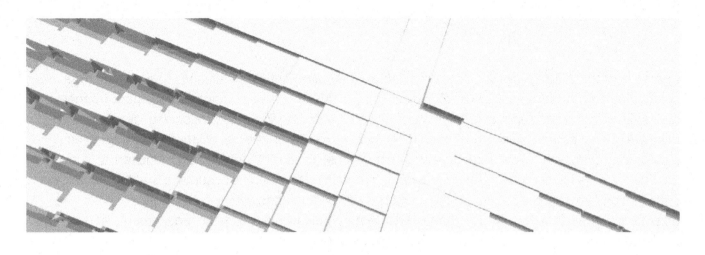

Chapter 8

Fieldwork Standards for Performance Audits

Learning objectives

- Recall key categories of performance audit objectives under generally accepted government auditing standards (GAGAS or the Yellow Book).

- Recognize three concepts related to the application of fieldwork standards in performance audits.

- Identify the 2018 Yellow Book fieldwork requirements for performance audits.

Introduction

Chapter 8 of the 2018 Yellow Book contains fieldwork requirements and guidance to assist auditors in conducting performance audits in accordance with GAGAS. This is necessary because performance audits differ from audits and reviews of financial statements and from attestation engagements and thus, are not encompassed in any of the AICPA auditing, review or attestation standards, though an auditor may choose to follow them if desired. The purpose of the GAGAS fieldwork requirements is to provide an overall approach for auditors to apply in obtaining reasonable assurance that the evidence is sufficient and appropriate to support the auditors' findings and conclusions based on the audit objectives. For performance audits conducted in accordance with GAGAS, the requirements and guidance in chapters 1–5, 8 and 9 of the 2018 Yellow Book apply.

This chapter presents the requirements related to fieldwork standards for performance audits. The concepts of evidence, significance, and audit risk form a framework for applying the requirements found in chapter 8 of GAGAS. Some of those requirements, and the related application guidance, are similar to those found in the GAGAS auditing standards. This chapter will focus on the application guidance that is specific to performance audits, and the unique characteristics of performance audits. Note that chapter 8 of GAGAS includes a significant amount of application guidance not included here. That information is a good resource when conducting a performance audit under GAGAS.

Performance audit objectives

Performance audits provide objective analysis, findings, and conclusions to assist management and those charged with governance and oversight with, among other things, improving program performance and operations, reducing costs, facilitating decision-making by parties responsible for overseeing or initiating corrective action, and contributing to public accountability. The scope of the audit objectives of performance audits can vary widely due to the nature of these engagements. Chapter 1 of GAGAS provides many examples of audit objectives for the categories that follow. Key categories of performance audit objectives, along with some examples of audit objectives for each category, include the following:

- Program effectiveness and results
  - Analyzing the relative cost-effectiveness of a program or activity
  - Determining whether a program produced intended results or produced results that were not consistent with the program's objectives
  - Evaluating whether the entity is following sound procurement practices
- Internal control
  - Resources are used in compliance with laws, regulations, or other requirements
  - Management information, such as performance measures, and public reports are complete, accurate, and consistent to support performance and decision-making
- Compliance
  - Government services and benefits are distributed or delivered to citizens based on eligibility to obtain those services and benefits
  - Revenues received are in compliance with applicable laws, regulations, contracts, or grant agreements

- Prospective analysis
  - Policy or legislative proposals, including advantages, disadvantages, and analysis of stakeholder views
  - Management's assumptions on which on which prospective information is based

Fieldwork requirements

Chapter 8 of the 2018 Yellow Book discusses fieldwork requirements and guidance for performance audits conducted in accordance with GAGAS. The fieldwork requirements for performance audits are grouped into five sections as follows:

- Planning
- Conducting the engagement
- Supervision
- Evidence
- Audit documentation

Planning

GAGAS divides specific guidance related to planning into the following areas:

- General planning requirements and guidance
- Auditor communication
- Investigations or legal proceedings
- Results of previous engagements
- Assigning auditors
- Preparing a written audit plan

General planning requirements and guidance

Paragraphs 8.03–8.07 of GAGAS	Requirements: General
	8.03 Auditors must adequately plan the work necessary to address the audit objectives. Auditors must document the audit plan.
	8.04 Auditors must plan the audit to reduce audit risk to an acceptably low level.
	8.05 In planning the audit, auditors should assess significance and audit risk. Auditors should apply these assessments to establish the scope and methodology for addressing the audit objectives. Planning is a continuous process throughout the audit.
	8.06 Auditors should design the methodology to obtain sufficient, appropriate evidence that provides a reasonable basis for findings and conclusions based on the audit objectives and to reduce audit risk to an acceptably low level.
	8.07 Auditors should identify and use suitable criteria based on the audit objectives.

The crux of a performance audit hinges on the audit objectives. *Audit objectives* are what the audit is intended to accomplish, and the objectives distinguish the audit subject matter and performance aspects to be included. Auditors can think of audit objectives as questions about the program that the auditors seek to answer based on evidence obtained and assessed against criteria. Audit objectives may also relate to the current status or condition of a program. The term *program* as used in GAGAS includes processes, projects, studies, policies, operations, activities, entities, and functions.

Once the audit objectives are determined, the auditor must determine the scope of the audit. The *scope of the audit* is tied directly to the audit objectives and is what defines the subject matter that the auditors will assess and report on, such as a particular program or aspect of a program, the necessary documents or records, the period of time reviewed, and the locations that will be included.

The *methodology* to be used in a performance audit describes the nature and extent of audit procedures for obtaining and analyzing audit evidence to address the audit objectives. The methodology is broken down into audit procedures, which represent the specific steps and tests that auditors will perform to achieve the audit objectives. The audit methodology is designed to provide sufficient appropriate evidence on which the auditors can base their findings and conclusions to ensure they are valid, accurate, appropriate, and complete with respect to the audit objectives.

GAGAS notes auditors may need to refine or adjust the audit objectives, scope, and methodology as work is performed. However, auditors may not have latitude to define or adjust the audit objectives or scope in situations where the audit objectives are established by statute or legislative oversight.

The auditors determine the nature of sufficient, appropriate evidence, as well as the tests of evidence needed to support the findings and conclusions based on the audit objectives. The objectives of performance audits may vary from the very narrow to the very broad. In some engagements, sufficient, appropriate evidence is available; however, in some cases the information may have limitations. Professional judgment is needed in determining whether audit evidence has been obtained that is sufficient to address the audit objectives.

Auditors are responsible for measuring or evaluating the subject matter of the engagement and for presenting the resulting information as part of, or accompanying, the audit report in a performance audit conducted in accordance with GAGAS. Therefore, GAGAS does not require auditors to obtain management assertions with respect to the subject matter when conducting a performance audit.

Auditors apply the concept of significance throughout a performance audit, including deciding the type and extent of audit work to perform, evaluating results of audit work, and developing the report and related findings and conclusions. *Significance* is defined as the relative importance of a matter within the context in which it is being considered, including quantitative and qualitative factors. Auditors should use professional judgment when evaluating the significance of matters within the context of the audit objectives.

> In the performance audit requirements, the term *significant* is comparable to the term *material* as used in the context of financial statement engagements.

In planning the audit, criteria should be identified as determined by the audit objectives. *Criteria* identify the required or desired state or expectation as it relates to the program or operation. It provides a context for evaluating evidence obtained, and understanding the findings, recommendations, and conclusions in the report. Criteria is suitable if it is relevant, reliable, objective, and understandable. Examples of criteria include the following:

- Laws and regulations
- Goals, policies, and procedures established by officials of the audited entity
- Technically developed standards or norms
- Expert opinions
- Prior period performance

- Defined business practices
- Contracts or grant agreements
- Benchmarks against which performance is compared

Auditor communication

Paragraphs 8.20–8.22 of GAGAS	Requirements: Auditor Communication
	8.20 Auditors should communicate an overview of the objectives, scope, and methodology and the timing of the performance audit and planned reporting (including any potential restrictions on the report), unless doing so could significantly impair the auditors' ability to obtain sufficient, appropriate evidence to address the audit objectives. Auditors should communicate such information with the following parties, as applicable: a. management of the audited entity, including those with sufficient authority and responsibility to implement corrective action in the program or activity being audited; b. those charged with governance; c. the individuals contracting for or requesting audit services, such as contracting officials or grantees; or d. the cognizant legislative committee, when auditors conduct the audit pursuant to a law or regulation or when they conduct the work for the legislative committee that has oversight of the audited entity. **8.21** In situations where the parties required to receive communications, as described in paragraph 8.20, are not clearly evident, auditors should document the process followed and conclusions reached in identifying the appropriate individuals to receive the required communications. **8.22** Auditors should retain any written communication resulting from paragraph 8.20 as audit documentation.

Examples of communications that may impair the auditor's ability to obtain sufficient audit evidence would include procedures such as unannounced cash counts or performing procedures related to indications of fraud.

The form and content of required communications are a matter of professional judgment, though GAGAS recommends that communications be made in writing, such as in an engagement letter.

Investigations or legal proceedings

Paragraph 8.27 of GAGAS	Requirements: Investigations or Legal Proceedings
	8.27 Auditors should inquire of management of the audited entity whether any investigations or legal proceedings significant to the audit objectives have been initiated or are in process with respect to the period under audit and should evaluate the effect of initiated or in-process investigations or legal proceedings on the current audit.

Auditors may be required to report certain indications of the following to law enforcement or investigatory agencies to maintain compliance with laws, regulations, or policies prior to performing additional audit procedures:

- Certain types of fraud
- Noncompliance with provisions of laws, regulations, contracts, and grant agreements

In a performance audit, as with other GAGAS engagements, avoiding any interference with investigations or legal proceedings when pursuing indications of fraud and noncompliance with provisions of laws, regulations, contracts, and grant agreements is a top priority. Thus, auditors may consider working with investigators or legal authorities or withdrawing from or deferring further work on the engagement or a portion of the engagement to avoid interfering with an ongoing investigation or legal proceeding.

Results of previous engagements

Paragraph 8.30 of GAGAS	Requirements: Results of Previous Engagements
	8.30 Auditors should evaluate whether the audited entity has taken appropriate corrective action to address findings and recommendations from previous engagements that are significant within the context of the audit objectives. When planning the audit, auditors should ask management of the audited entity to identify previous engagements or other studies that directly relate to the objectives of the audit, including whether related recommendations have been implemented. Auditors should use this information in assessing risk and determining the nature, timing, and extent of current audit work, including determining the extent to which testing the implementation of the corrective actions is applicable to the current audit objectives.

Assigning auditors

Paragraphs 8.31–8.32 of GAGAS	Requirements: Assigning Auditors
	8.31 Audit management should assign sufficient auditors with adequate collective professional competence, as described in paragraphs 4.02 through 4.15 of GAGAS, to conduct the audit. Staffing an audit includes, among other things, a. assigning auditors with the collective knowledge, skills, and abilities appropriate for the audit; b. assigning a sufficient number of auditors to the audit; c. providing for on-the-job training of auditors; and d. engaging specialists when necessary.
	8.32 If planning to use the work of specialists, auditors should document the nature and scope of the work to be performed by the specialists, including a. the objectives and scope of the specialists' work, b. the intended use of the specialists' work to support the audit objectives, c. the specialists' procedures and findings so they can be evaluated and related to other planned audit procedures, and d. the assumptions and methods used by the specialists.

Preparing a written audit plan

Paragraph 8.33 of GAGAS	Requirement: Preparing a Written Audit Plan
	8.33 Auditors must prepare a written audit plan for each audit. Auditors should update the plan, as necessary, to reflect any significant changes to the plan made during the audit.

The form and content of the auditors' written audit plan will likely vary among audits to reflect the differences in audit objectives. The auditor should consider tailoring the audit plan accordingly and should consider including items such as an audit strategy, audit program, project plan, audit planning paper, or other appropriate documentation of key decisions about the audit objectives, scope, and methodology and the auditors' basis for those decisions.

The purpose of a written audit plan is to allow the audit organization management to supervise audit planning and to evaluate whether

- the proposed audit objectives are likely to result in a useful report;
- the audit plan adequately addresses relevant risks;
- the proposed audit scope and methodology are adequate to address the audit objectives;

- available evidence is likely to be sufficient and appropriate for purposes of the audit; and
- sufficient staff, supervisors, and specialists with adequate collective professional competence and other resources are available to conduct the audit and to meet expected time frames for completing the work.

Knowledge check

1. The auditor must plan a performance audit in accordance with GAGAS to accomplish the following **except** to

    a. Obtain a low level of control risk.
    b. Reduce audit risk to an acceptably low level.
    c. Design the methodology to obtain sufficient, appropriate evidence.
    d. Identify and use suitable criteria based on the audit objectives.

Conducting the engagement

GAGAS provides guidance regarding the following nine components of conducting a performance audit:

- Nature and profile of the program and user needs
- Determining significance and obtaining an understanding of internal control
- Assessing internal control
- Internal control deficiencies considerations
- Information systems controls considerations
- Provisions of laws, regulations, contracts, and grant agreements
- Fraud
- Identifying sources of evidence and the amount and type of evidence required
- Using the work of others

Nature and profile of the program and user needs

Paragraph 8.36 of GAGAS	Requirement: Nature and Profile of the Program and User Needs
	8.36 Auditors should obtain an understanding of the nature of the program or program component under audit and the potential use that will be made of the audit results or report as they plan a performance audit. The nature and profile of a program include a. visibility, sensitivity, and relevant risks associated with the program under audit; b. age of the program or changes in its condition; c. the size of the program in terms of total dollars, number of citizens affected, or other measures; d. level and extent of review or other forms of independent oversight; e. the program's strategic plan and objectives; and f. external factors or conditions that could directly affect the program.

Users of a performance audit report may influence performance audit planning and conduct. Some relevant users may include

- government officials or other parties that authorized or requested the audit
- the audited entity and those responsible for acting on the results of the audit
- legislators or government officials
- the media
- interest groups, and
- individual citizens.

Potential users may have an ability to influence the conduct of the program as well as having an interest in the program. Therefore, awareness of the potential users' interest and influence may assist the auditor in determining whether possible findings could be significant to users.

GAGAS also requires that auditors gain an understanding of the nature and components of a program under audit. This process assists auditors to assess the relevant risks associated with the program and the effect of the risks on the audit objectives, scope, and methodology. In some cases, auditors already have knowledge about the program. In other cases, this understanding is obtained from inquiries, observations, and reviewing documents while planning the audit. The extent and breadth of those inquiries and observations varies by audit due to the difference between audit objectives, as does the need to understand individual aspects of the program, which may include the following:

- Provisions of laws, regulations, contracts, and grant agreements
- Purpose and goals of the program
- Internal control — plans, methods, policies, and procedures used to achieve the objectives of the entity
- Inputs — resources put into the program
- Program operations — strategies, processes, and activities of the program
- Outputs — the quantity or goods or services produced by a program
- Outcomes — accomplishments or results of a program

Determining significance and obtaining an understanding of internal control

Paragraphs 8.39–8.40 of GAGAS	Requirements: Determining Significance and Obtaining an Understanding of Internal Control
	8.39 Auditors should determine and document whether internal control is significant to the audit objectives.
	8.40 If it is determined that internal control is significant to the audit objectives, auditors should obtain an understanding of such internal control.

Internal control is not a significant element in all performance audits. Therefore, auditors need to gain an understanding of the audit objectives to determine whether internal control is significant. This determination should be documented. Evaluating the significance of internal control to the audit objectives includes consideration of the following factors:

- The subject matter under audit, such as the program or program component under audit, including the audited entity's objectives for the program and associated inherent risks
- The nature of findings and conclusions expected to be reported, based on the needs and interests of audit report users
- The three categories of entity objectives, that is operations, reporting, and compliance as defined by *Internal Control – Integrated Framework* (COSO Framework) and *Standards for Internal Control in the Federal Government* (Green Book)
- The five components of internal control (control environment, risk assessment, control activities, information and communication, and monitoring) and the integration of the components

If auditors determine that internal control is significant to the audit objectives, the next step is for auditors to decide which of the five components of internal control are significant to the audit objectives. Though all components of internal control are generally relevant, not all components may be considered significant to the audit objectives.

As the audit objectives evolve and become more refined throughout the audit, the significance of internal control on the audit objectives may necessitate reconsidering the prior conclusions reached.

Documentation of the significance of internal control may be in a variety of formats including narratives or tables. The documentation includes the conclusions on whether internal control is significant to the audit objectives, and if so, which components of internal control are significant to the audit objectives.

Audit planning is necessarily affected by the determination of the significance of internal control to the audit objectives. The significance level enables auditors to determine whether to assess internal control as part of the audit and, if so, to identify criteria for the assessment and plan the appropriate scope, methodology, and extent of internal control assessments to perform.

Professional judgment is used when establishing the nature and extent of procedures to perform to obtain an understanding of internal control. The nature and extent will likely vary among audits based on

- audit objectives,
- audit risk,
- internal control deficiencies, and
- the auditors' knowledge about internal control gained in prior audits.

Auditors may employ procedures such as inquiries, observations, inspection of documents and records, review of other audit reports, or direct tests to assist them in gaining an understanding of internal control.

To gain an understanding of internal controls, auditors may consider entity-level controls, transaction-level controls, or both. However, even when assessing only transaction-level controls, auditors may find it beneficial to gain an understanding of entity-level controls that may affect transaction-level controls by obtaining a broad understanding of the five components of internal control at the entity level. An understanding of the relationships between the components may be helpful.

In addition to obtaining a broad understanding of internal control at the entity level, auditors may also obtain an understanding of internal control at the transaction level for the specific programs and processes under audit. Obtaining an understanding of internal control assists auditors in identifying an audited entity's key controls relevant to the audit objectives.

Assessing internal control

Paragraph 8.49 of GAGAS	Requirement: Assessing Internal Control
	8.49 If internal control is determined to be significant to the audit objectives, auditors should assess and document their assessment of the design, implementation, and/or operating effectiveness of such internal control to the extent necessary to address the audit objectives.

Once an auditor determines that elements of internal control are significant to the audit objectives and has gained an understanding of the system of internal controls, GAGAS expects that the auditor will build on that understanding to further analyze and document an assessment of internal control.

The understanding of internal control gained by auditors provides a basis for determining the nature, timing, and extent of procedures necessary to assess internal control. The purpose of the assessment is to design and perform procedures to obtain sufficient, appropriate evidence to support and document the auditors' findings and conclusions on the design, implementation, and/or operating effectiveness of controls that are significant to the audit objectives. Auditors generally focus on assessing the key controls identified during the planning phase of the engagement, which may include controls at both the entity and transaction levels.

Depending on the results of the prior level's assessment, internal control may be assessed at one of the following levels:

- Design
- Design and implementation
- Design, implementation, and operating effectiveness

Auditors assess the design of internal control by determining whether controls individually and in combination are capable of achieving an objective and addressing the related risk. Auditors assess the implementation of internal control by establishing if the control exists and has been placed into operation. The operating effectiveness of internal control is assessed by determining whether controls were applied at relevant times during the period under evaluation, the consistency with which they were applied, and by whom or by what means they were applied. A control cannot be effectively implemented if it was not effectively designed and a control cannot operate effectively if it was not effectively designed and implemented.

The assessment of internal control may identify the following deficiencies:

- A deficiency in internal control exists when the design, implementation, or operation of a control does not allow management or personnel to achieve control objectives and address related risks.

- A deficiency in design exists when a necessary control is missing or is not properly designed so that even if the control operates as designed, the control objective would not be met.

- A deficiency in implementation exists when a control is properly designed but not implemented correctly in the internal control system.

- A deficiency in operating effectiveness exists when a properly designed control does not operate as designed or the person performing the control does not have the necessary competence or authority to perform the control effectively.

Internal control deficiencies considerations

Paragraph 8.54 of GAGAS	Requirement: Internal Control Deficiencies Considerations
	8.54 Auditors should evaluate and document the significance of identified internal control deficiencies within the context of the audit objectives.

The significance of deficiencies are evaluated both on an individual basis and in the aggregate, with consideration given to the correlation among deficiencies. The auditors' determination of whether, individually or in combination, the deficiencies are significant within the context of the audit objectives is made based on the audit work performed. Determining whether deficiencies are significant within the context of the audit objectives involves evaluating the magnitude of impact, likelihood of occurrence, and nature of the deficiency.

Because internal control deficiencies are a type of audit finding, auditors are required to plan and perform procedures to develop the criteria, condition, cause, and effect or potential effect of the findings to the extent that these elements are relevant and necessary to achieve the audit objectives. It may be helpful for auditors to perform an analysis to identify the root cause of the deficiencies because this may assist the auditor in recommending corrective actions.

Information systems controls considerations

Paragraphs 8.59–8.62 of GAGAS	Requirements: Information Systems Controls Considerations
	8.59 The effectiveness of significant internal controls frequently depends on the effectiveness of information systems controls. Thus, when obtaining an understanding of internal control significant to the audit objectives, auditors should also determine whether it is necessary to evaluate information systems controls.
	8.60 When information systems controls are determined to be significant to the audit objectives or when the effectiveness of significant controls depends on the effectiveness of information systems controls, auditors should then evaluate the design, implementation, and/or operating effectiveness of such controls. This evaluation includes other information systems controls that affect the effectiveness of the significant controls or the reliability of information used in performing the significant controls. Auditors should obtain a sufficient understanding of information systems controls necessary to assess audit risk and plan the audit within the context of the audit objectives.
	8.61 Auditors should determine which audit procedures related to information systems controls are needed to obtain sufficient, appropriate evidence to support the audit findings and conclusions.
	8.62 When evaluating information systems controls is an audit objective, auditors should test information systems controls to the extent necessary to address the audit objective.

Gaining an understanding of information systems controls as part of a performance audit is important when information systems are used extensively throughout the program under audit and the information systems are integral to the fundamental business processes related to the audit objectives. Information systems controls include those internal controls that depend on information systems processing and include general controls, application controls, and user controls.

Though an entity's use of information systems controls may be extensive, auditors are primarily interested in those information systems controls that are significant to the audit objectives. Auditors may employ procedures to evaluate the effectiveness of significant information systems controls such as

- gaining an understanding of the system as it relates to the information; and
- identifying and evaluating the general, application, and user controls that are critical to providing assurance over the reliability of the information required for the audit.

Depending on the audit's objectives, auditors may evaluate controls of information systems as part of the auditors' consideration of internal control. Auditors should exercise professional judgment when determining the extent of audit procedures necessary to obtain an understanding, depending on the significance of information systems controls to the audit objectives. When making the determination of the procedures to be performed, consideration is given to the nature and extent of audit risk related to information systems controls as they may be affected by the hardware and software used, the configuration of the entity's systems and networks, and the entity's information systems strategy.

Provisions of laws, regulations, contracts, and grant agreements

Paragraph 8.68 of GAGAS	Requirement: Provisions of Laws, Regulations, Contracts and Grant Agreements
	8.68 Auditors should identify any provisions of laws, regulations, contracts, and grant agreements that are significant within the context of the audit objectives and assess the risk that noncompliance with provisions of laws, regulations, contracts, and grant agreements could occur. Based on that risk assessment, the auditors should design and perform procedures to obtain reasonable assurance of detecting instances of noncompliance with provisions of laws, regulations, contracts, and grant agreements that are significant within the context of the audit objectives.

Although government programs are subject to many provisions of laws, regulations, contracts, and grant agreements, the significance of these provisions within the context of the audit objectives varies, depending on the objectives of the audit. Legal counsel and others, such as investigative staff, other audit organizations or government entities that provided professional services to the audited entity, or law enforcement authorities, may be consulted for information in determining those laws and regulations that are significant to the audit objectives, and other information to assist in design tests of compliance and evaluating the result of those tests.

The complexity or recent establishment of the laws, regulations, contracts, and grant agreements may affect the assessment of audit risk as well as by whether the audited entity has controls that are effective in preventing or detecting noncompliance with provisions of laws, regulations, contracts, and grant agreements. Tests of compliance may be reduced if auditors are able to obtain sufficient, appropriate evidence of the effectiveness of these controls.

Fraud

Paragraphs 8.71–8.72 of GAGAS	Requirements: Fraud
	8.71 Auditors should assess the risk of fraud occurring that is significant within the context of the audit objectives. Audit team members should discuss among the team fraud risks, including factors such as individuals' incentives or pressures to commit fraud, the opportunity for fraud to occur, and rationalizations or attitudes that could increase the risk of fraud. Auditors should gather and assess information to identify the risk of fraud that is significant within the scope of the audit objectives or that could affect the findings and conclusions.
	8.72 Assessing the risk of fraud is an ongoing process throughout the audit. When information comes to the auditors' attention indicating that fraud, significant within the context of the audit objectives, may have occurred, auditors should extend the audit steps and procedures, as necessary, to 1) determine whether fraud has likely occurred and 2) if so, determine its effect on the audit findings.

GAGAS defines *fraud* as obtaining something of value through willful misrepresentation. The judicial or other adjudicative system is responsible for determining whether an act is, in fact, fraud and GAGAS states that it is beyond auditors' professional responsibility. An attitude of professional skepticism is needed when assessing the risk of fraud and in assessing which factors or risks could significantly affect the audit objectives.

If the auditors identify fraud that is not significant within the context of the audit objectives, they may perform additional audit work as a separate engagement or refer the matter to other parties with oversight responsibility or jurisdiction.

Knowledge check

2. GAGAS identifies a number of primary users of performance audit reports. Which of the following is **not** one of these users?

    a. Management responsible for acting on audit results.
    b. Legislators and government officials.
    c. Media.
    d. Internal auditors.

3. Which of the following is an auditor **not** required to do when internal control is significant to the audit objectives in the performance audit?

   a. Obtain an understanding of all elements of internal controls related to the audit objectives.
   b. Obtain an understanding of internal control significant to the audit objectives.
   c. Assess and document the assessment of the design, implementation, and operating effectiveness of such internal control to the extent necessary to address the audit objectives.
   d. Evaluate and document the significance of identified internal control deficiencies within the context of the audit objectives.

Identifying sources of evidence and the amount and type of evidence required

Paragraphs 8.77–8.78 of GAGAS	Requirements: Identifying Sources of Evidence and the Amount and Type of Evidence Required
	8.77 Auditors should identify potential sources of information that could be used as evidence. Auditors should determine the amount and type of evidence needed to obtain sufficient, appropriate evidence to address the audit objectives and adequately plan audit work.
	8.78 Auditors should evaluate whether any lack of sufficient, appropriate evidence is caused by internal control deficiencies or other program weaknesses, and whether the lack of sufficient, appropriate evidence could be the basis for audit findings.

Auditors may need to revise the audit objectives or modify the scope and methodology and formulate alternative procedures to obtain additional evidence or other forms of evidence if they have reason to believe it is likely that sufficient, appropriate evidence will not be available to address the current audit objectives.

Using the work of others

GAGAS includes provisions to encourage auditors to avoid duplication of efforts by including requirements for auditors to evaluate whether other auditors, either internal or external, may have performed procedures relevant to the audit objectives that may be relied upon in their audits. Auditors should perform procedures as set forth in the GAGAS requirements to enable them to rely on other auditors' work if it is applicable to their current audit objectives.

Paragraphs 8.80–8.82 of GAGAS	Requirements: Using the Work of Others
	8.80 Auditors should determine whether other auditors have conducted, or are conducting, audits that could be relevant to the current audit objectives.
	8.81 If auditors use the work of other auditors, they should perform procedures that provide a sufficient basis for using that work.
	Auditors should obtain evidence concerning the other auditors' qualifications and independence and should determine whether the scope, quality, and timing of the audit work performed by the other auditors can be relied on in the context of the current audit objectives.
	8.82 If the engagement team intends to use the work of a specialist, it should assess the independence of the specialist.

Supervision

As with all types of GAGAS engagements, auditors are required to properly supervise the engagement staff. Audit supervision includes providing sufficient guidance and direction to staff to address the audit objectives and follow applicable requirements. Furthermore, proper supervision comprises staying informed about significant problems encountered, reviewing the work performed, and providing effective on-the-job training.

The nature and extent of the supervision and review of work will vary based on the size of the audit organization, the experience level of staff, and the significance of the work performed.

Paragraph 8.87 of GAGAS	Requirement: Supervision
	8.87 Auditors must properly supervise audit staff.

Evidence

Paragraphs 8.90–8.94 of GAGAS	Requirements: Evidence
	8.90 Auditors must obtain sufficient, appropriate evidence to provide a reasonable basis for addressing the audit objectives and supporting their findings and conclusions.
	8.91 In assessing the appropriateness of evidence, auditors should assess whether the evidence is relevant, valid, and reliable.
	8.92 In determining the sufficiency of evidence, auditors should determine whether enough appropriate evidence exists to address the audit objectives and support the findings and conclusions to the extent that would persuade a knowledgeable person that the findings are reasonable.
	8.93 When auditors use information provided by officials of the audited entity as part of their evidence, they should determine what the officials of the audited entity or other auditors did to obtain assurance over the reliability of the information.
	8.94 Auditors should evaluate the objectivity, credibility, and reliability of testimonial evidence.

Because evidence is the key to providing a reasonable basis supporting an auditor's findings and conclusions in a performance audit, GAGAS provides significant application guidance regarding audit evidence. This guidance includes information regarding determining and evaluating the sufficiency and appropriateness of audit evidence obtained. Appropriateness of audit evidence is discussed along with types of audit evidence and its reliability.

When entity officials provide information auditors use to support their findings and conclusions, auditors may find it necessary to test management's procedures, perform direct testing of the information, or obtain additional evidence. The additional nature, timing, and extent of such testing depends on the significance and nature of the information. Written representations may be deemed to be appropriate concerning the accuracy and completeness of the information provided.

Overall assessment of evidence

Paragraphs 8.108–8.110 of GAGAS	Requirements: Overall Assessment of Evidence
	8.108 Auditors should perform and document an overall assessment of the collective evidence used to support findings and conclusions, including the results of any specific assessments performed to conclude on the validity and reliability of specific evidence.
	8.109 When assessing the overall sufficiency and appropriateness of evidence, auditors should evaluate the expected significance of evidence to the audit objectives, findings, and conclusions; available corroborating evidence; and the level of audit risk. If auditors conclude that evidence is not sufficient or appropriate, they should not use such evidence as support for findings and conclusions.
	8.110 When the auditors identify limitations or uncertainties in evidence that is significant to the audit findings and conclusions, they should perform additional procedures, as appropriate.

Sufficiency and appropriateness of evidence are relative concepts and may be thought of as a continuum rather than as an absolute. Because both concepts are evaluated in the context of the related findings and conclusions, even though the auditors may identify some limitations or uncertainties about the sufficiency or appropriateness of some of the evidence, they may nonetheless determine that in total there is sufficient, appropriate evidence to support the findings and conclusions.

An auditor's process to assess evidence may depend on the nature of the evidence, how the evidence is used in the audit or report, and the audit objectives. Evidence is considered sufficient and appropriate when it provides a reasonable basis for supporting the findings or conclusions within the context of the audit objectives. However, it is not sufficient or appropriate when

- using the evidence carries an unacceptably high risk that it could lead auditors to reach an incorrect or improper conclusion;
- the evidence has significant limitations, given the audit objectives and intended use of the evidence; or
- the evidence does not provide an adequate basis for addressing the audit objectives or supporting the findings and conclusions.

Given the audit objectives and the intended use of the evidence, it is considered limited in use when its validity or reliability has not been assessed or cannot be assessed by the auditor. Limitations also include errors identified by the auditors in their testing.

To address limitations or uncertainties in evidence that are significant to the audit findings and conclusions, auditors may be able to effectively apply the following additional procedures:

- Seek independent, corroborating evidence from other sources
- Redefine the audit objectives or the audit scope to eliminate the need to use the evidence
- Presenting the findings and conclusions so that the supporting evidence is sufficient and appropriate and describe in the report the limitations or uncertainties with the validity or reliability of the evidence, if such disclosure is necessary to avoid misleading the report users about the findings or conclusions
- Determine whether to report the limitations or uncertainties as a finding, including any related significant internal control deficiencies.

Findings

Paragraphs 8.116–8.117 of GAGAS	Requirements: Findings
	8.116 As part of a performance audit, when auditors identify findings, they should plan and perform procedures to develop the criteria, condition, cause, and effect of the findings to the extent that these elements are relevant and necessary to achieve the audit objectives.
	8.117 Auditors should consider internal control deficiencies in their evaluation of identified findings when developing the cause element of the identified findings when internal control is significant to the audit objectives.

In a performance audit, findings identified may involve deficiencies in internal control, noncompliance with provisions of laws, regulations, contracts, and grant agreements, or instances of fraud. Much of the guidance related to findings identified in performance audits, including the definitions of criteria, condition, cause and effect, and waste and abuse, is similar to the guidance provided by GAGAS related to financial audits.

In a performance audit, however, the elements of criteria, condition, cause, and effect or potential effect needed for a finding are related to the objectives of the performance audit. Therefore, a finding or set of findings is complete to the extent that the audit objectives are addressed, and the report clearly relates those objectives to the elements of a finding. For instance, if an audit objective is to determine the current status or condition of program operations or progress in implementing legislative requirements, and not the related cause or effect, then developing the condition of the finding would address the audit objective and developing the other elements of a finding would not be necessary.

Audit documentation

Paragraphs 8.132–8.136 of GAGAS	Requirements: Audit Documentation
	8.132 Auditors must prepare audit documentation related to planning, conducting, and reporting for each audit. Auditors should prepare audit documentation in sufficient detail to enable an experienced auditor, having no previous connection to the audit, to understand from the audit documentation the nature, timing, extent, and results of audit procedures performed; the evidence obtained; and its source and the conclusions reached, including evidence that supports the auditors' significant judgments and conclusions.
	8.133 Auditors should prepare audit documentation that contains evidence that supports the findings, conclusions, and recommendations before they issue their report.
	8.134 Auditors should design the form and content of audit documentation to meet the circumstances of the particular audit. The audit documentation constitutes the principal record of the work that the auditors have performed in accordance with standards and the conclusions that the auditors have reached. The quantity, type, and content of audit documentation are a matter of the auditors' professional judgment.
	8.135 Auditors should document the following:
	a. the objectives, scope, and methodology of the audit;
	b. the work performed and evidence obtained to support significant judgments and conclusions, as well as expectations in analytical procedures, including descriptions of transactions and records examined (for example, by listing file numbers, case numbers, or other means of identifying specific documents examined, though copies of documents examined or detailed listings of information from those documents are not required); and
	c. supervisory review, before the audit report is issued, of the evidence that supports the findings, conclusions, and recommendations contained in the audit report.
	8.136 When auditors do not comply with applicable GAGAS requirements because of law, regulation, scope limitations, restrictions on access to records, or other issues affecting the audit, the auditors should document the departure from the GAGAS requirements and the impact on the audit and on the auditors' conclusions.

Availability of individuals and documentation

Paragraph 8.140 of GAGAS	Requirement: Availability of Individuals and Documentation
	8.140 Subject to applicable provisions of laws and regulations, auditors should make appropriate individuals and audit documentation available upon request and in a timely manner to other auditors or reviewers.

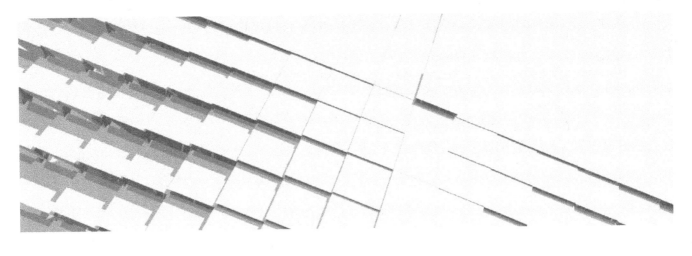

Chapter 9

Reporting Standards for Performance Audits

Learning objectives

- Identify the reporting requirements under generally accepted government auditing standards (GAGAS) for performance audits.

- Recognize the required contents of a performance audit report.

Introduction

Chapter 9 of GAGAS contains reporting requirements and guidance for performance audits conducted in accordance with GAGAS. The reporting requirements provide a comprehensive approach for auditors to use when communicating the results of the performance audit.

For performance audits conducted in accordance with GAGAS, the requirements and guidance in chapters 1–5, and 8 of the Yellow Book also apply.

The reporting requirements for performance audits include the following:

- Reporting auditors' compliance with GAGAS
- Report format
- Report content, including
    - Reporting findings, conclusions, and recommendations
    - Reporting on internal control

- – Reporting on noncompliance with provisions of laws, regulations, contracts, and grant agreements
- – Reporting on instances of fraud
- – Reporting findings directly to parties outside the audited entity
- Obtaining the views of responsible officials
- Report distribution
- Reporting confidential or sensitive information
- Discovery of insufficient evidence after report release

Reporting on auditors' compliance with GAGAS

Paragraphs 9.03–9.05 of GAGAS	Requirements: Reporting the Auditors' Compliance with GAGAS
	9.03 When auditors comply with all applicable GAGAS requirements, they should use the following language, which represents an unmodified GAGAS compliance statement, in the audit report to indicate that they conducted the audit in accordance with GAGAS:
	We conducted this performance audit in accordance with generally accepted government auditing standards. Those standards require that we plan and perform the audit to obtain sufficient, appropriate evidence to provide a reasonable basis for our findings and conclusions based on our audit objectives. We believe that the evidence obtained provides a reasonable basis for our findings and conclusions based on our audit objectives.
	9.04 Audit organizations that meet the independence requirements for internal audit organizations, but not those for external audit organizations, should include in the GAGAS compliance statement, where applicable, a statement that they are independent per the GAGAS requirements for internal auditors.
	9.05 When auditors do not comply with all applicable GAGAS requirements, they should include a modified GAGAS compliance statement in the audit report. For performance audits, auditors should use a statement that includes either (1) the language in paragraph 9.03, modified to indicate the requirements that were not followed, or (2) language indicating that the auditors did not follow GAGAS.

Report format

Paragraphs 9.06–9.07 of GAGAS	Requirements: Report Format
	9.06 Auditors should issue audit reports communicating the results of each completed performance audit.
	9.07 Auditors should issue the audit report in a form that is appropriate for its intended use, either in writing or in some other retrievable form.

The purpose of the audit report is to

- clearly communicate the results of audits to those charged with governance, the appropriate officials of the audited entity, and the appropriate oversight officials and
- facilitate follow-up to determine whether appropriate corrective actions have been taken.

Auditors of performance audits have flexibility in the format of the report that they issue. The form of the audit report can be tailored to the users' needs. Different forms of audit reports include written reports, letters, briefing slides, or other presentation materials. Auditors may present audit reports using electronic media through which report users and the audit organization can retrieve them.

Report content

Paragraphs 9.10–9.14 of GAGAS	Requirements: Report Content
	9.10 Auditors should prepare audit reports that contain (1) the objectives, scope, and methodology of the audit; (2) the audit results, including findings, conclusions, and recommendations, as appropriate; (3) a summary of the views of responsible officials; and (4) if applicable, the nature of any confidential or sensitive information omitted.
	9.11 Auditors should communicate audit objectives in the audit report in a clear, specific, neutral, and unbiased manner that includes relevant assumptions. In order to avoid potential misunderstanding, when audit objectives are limited but users could infer broader objectives, auditors should state in the audit report that certain issues were outside the scope of the audit.
	9.12 Auditors should describe the scope of the work performed and any limitations, including issues that would be relevant to likely users, so that report users can reasonably interpret the findings, conclusions, and recommendations in the report without being misled. Auditors should also report any significant constraints imposed on the audit approach by information limitations or scope impairments, including denials of, or excessive delays in, access to certain records or individuals.
	9.13 In describing the work performed to address the audit objectives and support the reported findings and conclusions, auditors should, as applicable, explain the relationship between the population and the items tested; identify entities, geographic locations, and the period covered; report the kinds and sources of evidence; and explain any significant limitations or uncertainties based on the auditors' overall assessment of the sufficiency and appropriateness of the evidence in the aggregate.
	9.14 In reporting audit methodology, auditors should explain how the completed audit work supports the audit objectives, including the evidence-gathering and evidence-analysis techniques, in sufficient detail to allow knowledgeable users of their reports to understand how the auditors addressed the audit objectives. Auditors should identify significant assumptions made in conducting the audit; describe comparative techniques applied; describe the criteria used; and, when the results of sample testing significantly support the auditors' findings, conclusions, or recommendations, describe the sample design and state why the design was chosen, including whether the results can be projected to the intended population.

The users of performance audit reports need information regarding the audit objectives, scope, and methodology to understand the purpose of the audit; the nature and extent of the audit work performed;

the context and perspective regarding what is reported; and any significant limitations in the audit objectives, scope, or methodology. Therefore, GAGAS has provided guidance and requirements to ensure that the users of the reports have adequate information to make decisions and facilitate corrective actions where necessary. Although GAGAS specifies the elements to be contained within the report, auditors have discretion in the way in which the information is communicated.

The following report quality elements are important when developing and writing the audit report.

Accurate

GAGAS defines an *accurate report* as being supported by sufficient, appropriate evidence with key facts, figures, and findings being directly linked to the audit evidence obtained. Accuracy is facilitated by reports that are fact-based, with a clear statement of sources, methods, and assumptions so that report users can judge how much weight to give the evidence reported. Reports are also more accurate when auditors disclose data limitations in addition to other disclosures, as appropriate, and when the findings are presented in the broader context of the issue.

Using a quality control process, such as referencing the findings and conclusions back to the audit evidence, is one way to help the audit organization prepare accurate audit reports. Referencing is a process in which an experienced auditor, who is independent of the audit, verifies back to the audit work papers that statements of facts, figures, and dates are correctly reported; the findings are adequately supported by the evidence in the audit documentation; and the conclusions and recommendations flow logically from the evidence.

Objective

A report is considered objective when it is balanced in content and tone. The credibility of the report is considerably improved when it presents evidence in an unbiased manner and in the proper context. This includes presenting the audit results in an impartial and fair manner. Decision makers are more likely to act on the auditors' findings and recommendations based on a balanced tone of a report that presents sufficient, appropriate evidence to support conclusions and refrains from using adjectives or adverbs that characterize conclusions. The objectivity of a report is heightened when the report explicitly states the source of the evidence and the assumptions used in the analysis. This does not preclude the report from recognizing the positive aspects of the program reviewed if they are applicable to the audit objectives. Disclosing positive program aspects may lead to improved performance and implementation of best practices by other government organizations that read the report. Objective audit reports demonstrate that the work has been performed by professional, unbiased, independent, and knowledgeable personnel.

Complete

Completeness means that the report contains the sufficient, appropriate evidence needed to satisfy the audit objectives and promote an understanding to users of the matters reported. Additionally, it precludes omission of significant relevant information related to the evidence and findings related to the audit objectives. Including in the report information to provide perspective on the extent and significance of reported findings — such as the frequency of occurrence relative to the number of cases or transactions tested and the relationship of the findings to the entity's operations — will assist users in understanding the report. A complete report also clearly states what was and was not done and explicitly discloses data limitations, constraints imposed by restrictions on access to records, or other issues.

Convincing

A convincing report is one where the audit results are directly tied to the audit objectives, the findings are presented persuasively, and the conclusions and recommendations flow logically from the facts presented. The validity of the findings, the reasonableness of the conclusions, and the benefit of implementing the recommendations are more convincing when supported by sufficient, appropriate evidence. The benefit of a convincing report is that it can help focus the attention of responsible officials on the matters that are the most important and can provide an incentive for taking corrective action.

Clear

A clear report is easy for the intended user to read and understand. Using as clear and simple language as possible in the report helps auditors communicate with those charged with governance. A report should use straightforward, nontechnical language, and define technical terms, abbreviations, and acronyms that are used in the report. Auditors may choose to use a highlights page or summary within the report to capture the report user's attention and highlight the overall message. When using a summary, auditors may consider focusing on the audit objectives, summarizing the audit's most significant findings and the report's principal conclusions, and preparing users to anticipate the major recommendations. A clear and understandable report will be logically organized, contain accurate and precise facts and conclusions, and effectively use titles, captions and topic sentences to make the report easier to read and understand. Visual aids (such as pictures, charts, graphs, and maps) may also be helpful to summarize complex material.

Concise

Being concise means that the report is no longer than necessary to convey and support the message. Too much detail may detract from, confuse, or even conceal the real message being conveyed. Although the content of reports is subject to considerable professional judgment, those that are fact-based and concise are likely to achieve the best results.

Timely

To maximize effectiveness, the goal is to provide a report containing relevant evidence in time for users to respond to the needs of officials of the audited entity, legislative officials, and other users. Therefore, the timely issuance of the report is an important reporting target for auditors. To facilitate this objective, the auditors are encouraged to provide interim reports of significant matters to appropriate entity and oversight officials during the audit. Such communication alerts officials to matters needing immediate attention and allows them to take corrective action before the final report is completed.

Knowledge check

1. The following are all true related to the performance audit report, **except**

   a. Communicating the results of audits to those charged with governance, the appropriate officials of the audited entity, and the appropriate oversight officials is a purpose of the report.
   b. Facilitating follow-up to determine whether appropriate corrective actions have been taken is a purpose of the report.
   c. Audit reports may be in the form of written reports, letters, or briefing slides.
   d. Publishing the report electronically for users of the financial statements is a requirement.

2. The following are required to be included in a performance audit report **except** for

   a. The nature of any confidential or sensitive information omitted from the report.
   b. A statement whether any fraud was identified.
   c. The audit results, including findings.
   d. The objectives, scope, and methodology of the audit.

Reporting findings, conclusions, and recommendations

Paragraphs 9.18–9.23 of GAGAS	Requirements: Reporting Findings, Conclusions, and Recommendations
	9.18 In the audit report, auditors should present sufficient, appropriate evidence to support the findings and conclusions in relation to the audit objectives. Auditors should provide recommendations for corrective action if findings are significant within the context of the audit objectives.
	9.19 Auditors should report conclusions based on the audit objectives and the audit findings.
	9.20 Auditors should describe in their report limitations or uncertainties with the reliability or validity of evidence if (1) the evidence is significant to the findings and conclusions within the context of the audit objectives and (2) such disclosure is necessary to avoid misleading the report users about the findings and conclusions. Auditors should describe the limitations or uncertainties regarding evidence in conjunction with the findings and conclusions, in addition to describing those limitations or uncertainties as part of the objectives, scope, and methodology.
	9.21 Auditors should place their findings in perspective by describing the nature and extent of the issues being reported and the extent of the work performed that resulted in the findings. To give the reader a basis for judging the prevalence and consequences of these findings, auditors should, as appropriate, relate the instances identified to the population or the number of cases examined and quantify the results in terms of dollar value or other measures. If the results cannot be projected, auditors should limit their conclusions appropriately.

9.22 When reporting on the results of their work, auditors should disclose significant facts relevant to the objectives of their work and known to them that if not disclosed could mislead knowledgeable users, misrepresent the results, or conceal significant improper or illegal practices.

9.23 When feasible, auditors should recommend actions to correct deficiencies and other findings identified during the audit and to improve programs and operations when the potential for improvement in programs, operations, and performance is substantiated by the reported findings and conclusions. Auditors should make recommendations that flow logically from the findings and conclusions, are directed at resolving the cause of identified deficiencies and findings, and clearly state the actions recommended.

The audit objectives govern the extent to which the elements for a finding require development. When auditors clearly develop findings, it helps management and oversight officials to understand the need for taking corrective action.

Describing limitations regarding uncertainty about the sufficiency or appropriateness of some of the evidence provides report users with a clear understanding of how much responsibility the auditors are taking for the information.

GAGAS provides auditors flexibility in reporting so they may provide relevant contextual information to communicate the overall message, and to assist the reader in understanding the findings and significance of the issues disclosed. Auditors may choose to include background information such as information on how programs and operations work; the significance of programs and operations (for example, dollars, effect, purposes, and past audit work, if relevant); a description of the audited entity's responsibilities; and explanation of terms, organizational structure, and the statutory basis for the program and operations.

When reporting conclusions, auditors are not providing merely a summary of the findings. Instead, the conclusions are logical extrapolations about the program based on their findings. The potency of the auditors' conclusions is contingent on the persuasiveness of the evidence supporting the findings and the strength of the logic used to formulate the conclusions. Compelling conclusions lead to recommendations that persuade a knowledgeable user that action is necessary.

Effective recommendations will assist in encouraging improvements in the conduct of government programs and operations. Recommendations are effective when they are addressed to parties with the authority to act and when the recommended actions are specific, feasible, cost-effective, and measurable.

Reporting on internal control

Paragraphs 9.29–9.31 of GAGAS	Requirements: Reporting on Internal Control
	9.29 When internal control is significant within the context of the audit objectives, auditors should include in the audit report (1) the scope of their work on internal control and (2) any deficiencies in internal control that are significant within the context of the audit objectives and based upon the audit work performed.
	9.30 If some but not all internal control components are significant to the audit objectives, the auditors should identify as part of the scope those internal control components and underlying principles that are significant to the audit objectives.
	9.31 When auditors detect deficiencies in internal control that are not significant to the objectives of the audit but warrant the attention of those charged with governance, they should include those deficiencies either in the report or communicate those deficiencies in writing to audited entity officials. If the written communication is separate from the audit report, auditors should refer to that written communication in the audit report.

Although GAGAS requires that only significant internal control components be identified as part of the scope, auditors may include control components and underlying principles that are not considered significant to the audit objectives if, in their professional judgment, doing so is necessary to prevent a misunderstanding of the extensiveness of the conclusions of the audit report and to clarify that control effectiveness has not been evaluated as a whole. Auditors are also permitted to identify and describe the five components of internal control so that report users understand the scope of the work within the context of the entity's internal control system.

If the five components of internal control are effectively designed, implemented, and operating, and are well integrated, then an internal control system is considered to be effective. The principles of each component of internal control support the effective design, implementation, and operation of the associated components and represent conditions necessary to establish an effective internal control system. If one of the principles is not functioning properly, then the respective component cannot be effective. If a principle or component is not effective, or the components are not operating cohesively, then an internal control system cannot be effective.

Professional judgment is used when deciding whether and how to communicate to audited entity officials when they identify deficiencies in internal control that do not warrant the attention of those charged with governance.

Reporting on noncompliance with provisions of laws, regulations, contracts, and grant agreements

Paragraphs 9.35–9.36 of GAGAS	Requirements: Reporting on Noncompliance with Provisions of Laws, Regulations, Contracts, and Grant Agreements
	9.35 Auditors should report a matter as a finding when they conclude, based on sufficient, appropriate evidence, that noncompliance with provisions of laws, regulations, contracts, and grant agreements either has occurred or is likely to have occurred that is significant within the context of the audit objectives.
	9.36 Auditors should communicate findings in writing to audited entity officials when the auditors detect instances of noncompliance with provisions of laws, regulations, contracts, and grant agreements that are not significant within the context of the audit objectives but warrant the attention of those charged with governance.

Auditors are charged with reporting suspected or identified noncompliance under GAGAS. However, the actual determination about whether a particular act is, in fact, noncompliance with provisions of laws, regulations, contracts, and grant agreements may have to be determined by a court of law or other adjudicative body.

Professional judgment is used when deciding whether and how to communicate to audited entity officials any identified instances of noncompliance with provisions of laws, regulations, contracts, and grant agreements that do not warrant the attention of those charged with governance.

When noncompliance with provisions of laws, regulations, contracts, and grant agreements has occurred or is likely to have occurred, auditors may want to consult with authorities or legal counsel about whether publicly reporting such information would compromise investigative or legal proceedings.

GAGAS permits auditors to limit their public reporting to matters that would not compromise those proceedings and, for instance, report only on information that is already a part of the public record.

Reporting on instances of fraud

Reporting on instances of fraud is similar to that of reporting noncompliance with provisions of laws, regulations, contracts, and grant agreements.

Paragraphs 9.40–9.41 of GAGAS	Requirements: Reporting on Instances of Fraud
	9.40 Auditors should report a matter as a finding when they conclude, based on sufficient, appropriate evidence, that fraud either has occurred or is likely to have occurred that is significant to the audit objectives.

Paragraphs 9.40–9.41 of GAGAS	Requirements: Reporting on Instances of Fraud (continued)
	9.41 Auditors should communicate findings in writing to audited entity officials when the auditors detect instances of fraud that are not significant within the context of the audit objectives but warrant the attention of those charged with governance.

Reporting on findings directly to parties outside the audited entity

Paragraphs 9.45–9.47 of GAGAS	Requirements: Reporting Findings Directly to Parties Outside the Audited Entity
	9.45 Auditors should report known or likely noncompliance with provisions of laws, regulations, contracts, and grant agreements or fraud directly to parties outside the audited entity in the following two circumstances.
	a. When audited entity management fails to satisfy legal or regulatory requirements to report such information to external parties specified in law or regulation, auditors should first communicate the failure to report such information to those charged with governance. If the audited entity still does not report this information to the specified external parties as soon as practicable after the auditors' communication with those charged with governance, then the auditors should report the information directly to the specified external parties.
	b. When audited entity management fails to take timely and appropriate steps to respond to noncompliance with provisions of laws, regulations, contracts, and grant agreements or instances of fraud that (1) are likely to have a significant effect on the subject matter and (2) involve funding received directly or indirectly from a government agency, auditors should first report management's failure to take timely and appropriate steps to those charged with governance. If the audited entity still does not take timely and appropriate steps as soon as practicable after the auditors' communication with those charged with governance, then the auditors should report the audited entity's failure to take timely and appropriate steps directly to the funding agency.
	9.46 Auditors should comply with the requirements in paragraph 9.45 even if they have resigned or been dismissed from the audit prior to its completion.
	9.47 Auditors should obtain sufficient, appropriate evidence, such as confirmation from outside parties, to corroborate representations by audited entity management that it has reported audit findings in accordance with provisions of laws, regulations, or funding agreements. When auditors are unable to do so, they should report such information directly, as discussed in paragraphs 9.45 and 9.46.

GAGAS notes that these requirements are in addition to any legal requirements to report such information directly to parties outside the audited entity that the auditors may identify. Additionally, internal audit organizations are not required to report outside the audited entity unless required by law, regulation, or policy. These requirements mirror the requirements for reporting directly to parties outside of the entity in other types of GAGAS engagements.

Obtaining the views of responsible officials

Paragraphs 9.50–9.53 of GAGAS	Requirements: Obtaining the Views of Responsible Officials
	9.50 Auditors should obtain and report the views of responsible officials of the audited entity concerning the findings, conclusions, and recommendations in the audit report, as well as any planned corrective actions.
	9.51 When auditors receive written comments from the responsible officials, they should include in their report a copy of the officials' written comments or a summary of the comments received. When the responsible officials provide oral comments only, auditors should prepare a summary of the oral comments, provide a copy of the summary to the responsible officials to verify that the comments are accurately represented, and include the summary in their report.
	9.52 When the audited entity's comments are inconsistent or in conflict with the findings, conclusions, or recommendations in the draft report, the auditors should evaluate the validity of the audited entity's comments. If the auditors disagree with the comments, they should explain in the report their reasons for disagreement. Conversely, the auditors should modify their report as necessary if they find the comments valid and supported by sufficient, appropriate evidence.
	9.53 If the audited entity refuses to provide comments or is unable to provide comments within a reasonable period of time, the auditors may issue the report without receiving comments from the audited entity. In such cases, the auditors should indicate in the report that the audited entity did not provide comments.

As with other types of GAGAS engagements, GAGAS recommends providing a draft report with findings for review and comment by responsible officials of the audited entity and others to help the auditors develop a report that is fair, complete, and objective. Including the views of responsible officials leads to a report that presents not only the auditors' findings, conclusions, and recommendations but also the perspectives of the audited entity's responsible officials and the corrective actions they plan to take. It is preferable to obtain the comments in writing though oral comments are acceptable. Auditors may disclose in the report that technical comments were received in cases where the audited entity provided them in addition to their written or oral comments. Technical comments address points of fact or are editorial in nature and do not address substantive issues, such as methodology, findings, conclusions, or recommendations.

It is appropriate to obtain oral comments for a performance audit in the same circumstances as discussed with respect to other GAGAS engagements.

Report distribution

For purposes of making an audit report available to the public, auditors of external audit organizations may post the audit report to their publicly accessible websites or verify that the audited entity has posted the audit report to its publicly accessible website.

Paragraphs 9.56–9.59 of GAGAS	**Requirements: Report Distribution**
	9.56 Distribution of reports completed in accordance with GAGAS depends on the auditors' relationship with the audited organization and the nature of the information contained in the reports. Auditors should document any limitation on report distribution. Auditors should make audit reports available to the public, unless distribution is specifically limited by the terms of the engagement, law, or regulation.
	Report Distribution for Internal Auditors
	9.57 If an internal audit organization in a government entity follows the Institute of Internal Auditors' *International Standards for the Professional Practice of Internal Auditing* as well as GAGAS, the head of the internal audit organization should communicate results to the parties who can ensure that the results are given due consideration. If not otherwise mandated by statutory or regulatory requirements, prior to releasing results to parties outside the organization, the head of the internal audit organization should (1) assess the potential risk to the organization, (2) consult with senior management or legal counsel as appropriate, and (3) control dissemination by indicating the intended users in the report.
	Report Distribution for External Auditors
	9.58 An audit organization in a government entity should distribute audit reports to those charged with governance, to the appropriate audited entity officials, and to the appropriate oversight bodies or organizations requiring or arranging for the audits. As appropriate, auditors should also distribute copies of the reports to other officials who have legal oversight authority or who may be responsible for acting on audit findings and recommendations and to others authorized to receive such reports.
	9.59 A public accounting firm contracted to conduct an audit in accordance with GAGAS should clarify report distribution responsibilities with the engaging party. If the contracting firm is responsible for the distribution, it should reach agreement with the party contracting for the audit about which officials or organizations will receive the report and the steps being taken to make the report available to the public.

Reporting confidential or sensitive information

Paragraphs 9.61–9.63 of GAGAS	Requirements: Reporting Confidential or Sensitive Information
	9.61 If certain information is prohibited from public disclosure or is excluded from a report because of its confidential or sensitive nature, auditors should disclose in the report that certain information has been omitted and the circumstances that make the omission necessary.
	9.62 When circumstances call for omission of certain information, auditors should evaluate whether this omission could distort the audit results or conceal improper or illegal practices and revise the report language as necessary to avoid report users drawing inappropriate conclusions from the information presented.
	9.63 When the audit organization is subject to public records laws, auditors should determine whether public records laws could affect the availability of classified or limited use reports and determine whether other means of communicating with management and those charged with governance would be more appropriate. Auditors use judgment to determine the appropriate means to communicate the omitted information to management and those charged with governance considering, among other things, whether public records laws could affect the availability of classified or limited use reports.

Any reference within the report to omitted information may be general and not specific. Information not necessary to meet the audit objectives does not need to be referenced within the report.

Federal, state, or local laws or regulations may prohibit public disclosure of certain classified or otherwise prohibited information. In such circumstances, auditors may issue a separate, classified, or limited use report containing that information and distribute the report only to persons authorized by law or regulation to receive it.

As with examination and financial statement audits under GAGAS, there may be circumstances involving public safety, privacy, or security concerns that could justify the exclusion of certain information from a publicly available or widely distributed report.

In these circumstances, auditors may issue a limited use report containing such information and distribute the report only to those parties responsible for acting on the auditors' recommendations. The auditor may consider if it may be appropriate to issue both a publicly available report with the sensitive information excluded and a limited use report. GAGAS recommends that auditors consult with legal counsel regarding any requirements or other circumstances that may necessitate omitting certain information. Considering the broad public interest in the program or activity under audit assists when deciding whether to exclude certain information from publicly available reports.

Discovery of insufficient evidence after report release

Paragraph 9.68 of GAGAS	Requirement: Discovery of Insufficient Evidence after Report Release
	9.68 If, after the report is issued, the auditors discover that they did not have sufficient, appropriate evidence to support the reported findings or conclusions, they should communicate in the same manner as that used to originally distribute the report to those charged with governance, the appropriate officials of the audited entity, the appropriate officials of the entities requiring or arranging for the audits, and other known users, so that they do not continue to rely on the findings or conclusions that were not supported. If the report was previously posted to the auditors' publicly accessible website, the auditors should remove the report and post a public notification that the report was removed. The auditors should then determine whether to perform the additional audit work necessary to either reissue the report, including any revised findings or conclusions, or repost the original report if the additional audit work does not result in a change in findings or conclusions.

Knowledge check

3. Which statement is true regarding reporting on internal control in a performance audit?

    a. Deficiencies in internal control that are significant to the audit objectives should be reported.
    b. Reporting on internal control in a performance audit is not required unless an opinion is being issued.
    c. All internal control components are part of the consideration of reporting on internal control.
    d. Deficiencies in internal control are not required to be communicated to those changed with governance.

Exempt Organizations Glossary

Governmental terminology

accounting system. The methods and records established to identify, assemble, analyze, classify, record, and report a government's transactions and to maintain accountability for the related assets and liabilities.

accrual basis of accounting. The recording of financial effects on a government of transactions and other events and circumstances that have consequences for the government in the periods in which those transactions, events, and circumstances occur, rather than only in the periods in which cash is received or paid by the government.

ad valorem tax. A tax based on value (such as a property tax).

advance from other funds. An asset account used to record noncurrent portions of a long-term debt owed by one fund to another fund within the same reporting entity. (See **due to other funds** and **interfund receivable/payable**).

appropriation. A legal authorization granted by a legislative body to make expenditures and to incur obligations for specific purposes. An appropriation is usually limited in the amount and time it may be expended.

assigned fund balance. A portion of fund balance that includes amounts that are constrained by the government's intent to be used for specific purposes, but that are neither restricted nor committed.

basis of accounting. A term used to refer to *when* revenues, expenditures, expenses, and transfers, and related assets and liabilities are recognized in the accounts and reported in the financial statements. Specifically, it relates to the timing of the measurements made, regardless of the nature of the measurement. (See **accrual basis of accounting, cash basis of accounting,** and **modified accrual basis of accounting**).

bond. A written promise to pay a specified sum of money (the face value or principal amount) at a specified date or dates in the future (the maturity dates[s]), together with periodic interest at a specified rate. Sometimes, however, all or a substantial part of the interest is included in the face value of the security. The difference between a note and bond is that the latter is issued for a longer period and requires greater legal formality.

business type activities. Those activities of a government carried out primarily to provide specific services in exchange for a specific user charge.

capital grants. Grants restricted by the grantor for the acquisition or construction, or both, of capital assets.

capital projects fund. A fund used to account for and report financial resources that are restricted, committed, or assigned to expenditures for capital outlays, including the acquisition or construction of capital facilities and other capital assets. Capital project funds exclude those types of capital-related outflows financed by proprietary funds or for assets that will be held in trust for individuals, private organizations, or other governments.

cash basis of accounting. A basis of accounting that requires the recognition of transactions only when cash is received or disbursed.

committed fund balance. A portion of fund balance that includes amounts that can only be used for specific purposes pursuant to constraints imposed by formal action of the government's highest level of decision-making authority.

consumption method. The method of accounting that requires the recognition of an expenditure or expense as inventories are used.

contributed capital. Contributed capital is created when a general capital asset is transferred to a proprietary fund or when a grant is received that is externally restricted to capital acquisition or construction. Contributions restricted to capital acquisition and construction and capital assets received from developers are reported in the operating statement as a separate item after nonoperating revenues and expenses.

custodial fund. A fiduciary fund used to account for financial resources not administered through a trust or equivalent arrangement meeting specified criteria, and that are not required to be reported in a pension (and other employee benefit) trust fund, investment trust fund, or private-purpose trust fund.

debt service fund. A fund used to account for and report financial resources that are restricted, committed, or assigned to expenditure for principal and interest. Debt service funds should be used to report resources if legally mandated. Financial resources that are being accumulated for principal and interest maturing in future years should also be reported as debt service funds.

deferred inflow of resources. An acquisition of net assets by a government that is applicable to a future reporting period.

deferred outflow of resources. A consumption of net asset by a government that is applicable to a future reporting period.

deficit. (*a*) The excess of the liabilities of a fund over its assets. (*b*) The excess of expenditures over revenues during an accounting period or, in the case of proprietary funds, the excess of expenses over revenues during an accounting period.

disbursement. A payment made in cash or by check. Expenses are only recognized at the time physical cash is disbursed.

due from other funds. A current asset account used to indicate an account reflecting amounts owed to a particular fund by another fund for goods sold or services rendered. This account includes only short-term obligations on an open account, not interfund loans.

due to other funds. A current liability account reflecting amounts owed by a particular fund to another fund for goods sold or services rendered. This account includes only short-term obligations on an open account, not interfund loans.

enabling legislation. Legislation that authorizes a government to assess, levy, charge, or otherwise mandate payment of resources from external resource providers and includes a legally enforceable requirement that those resources be used for the specific purposes stipulated in the legislation.

encumbrances. Commitments related to unperformed (executory) contracts for goods or services. Used in budgeting, encumbrances are not generally accepted accounting principles (GAAP) expenditures or liabilities but represent the estimated amount of expenditures that will ultimately result if unperformed contracts in process are completed.

enterprise fund. A fund established to account for operations financed and operated in a manner similar to private business enterprises (such as gas, utilities, transit systems, and parking garages). Usually, the governing body intends that costs of providing goods or services to the general public be recovered primarily through user charges.

expenditures. Decreases in net financial resources. Expenditures include current operating expenses requiring the present or future use of net current assets, debt service and capital outlays, intergovernmental grants, entitlements, and shared revenues.

expenses. Outflows or other consumption of assets or incurrences of liabilities, or a combination of both, from delivering or producing goods, rendering services, or carrying out other activities that constitute the entity's ongoing major or central operations.

fiduciary fund. A fund that reports fiduciary activities meeting the criteria in paragraphs 6–11 of GASB Statement No. 84, *Fiduciary Activities*. Financial reporting is focused on reporting net position and changes in net position.

fund. A fiscal and accounting entity with a self-balancing set of accounts in which cash and other financial resources, all related liabilities and residual equities, or balances, and changes therein, are recorded and segregated to carry on specific activities or attain certain objectives in accordance with special regulations, restrictions, or limitations.

fund balance. The difference between fund assets and fund liabilities of the generic fund types within the governmental category of funds.

fund financial statements. Each fund has its own set of self-balancing accounts and fund financial statements that focus on information about the government's governmental, proprietary, and fiduciary fund types.

fund type. The 11 generic funds that all transactions of a government are recorded into. The 11 fund types are as follows: general, special revenue, debt service, capital projects, permanent, enterprise, internal service, private-purpose trust, pension (and other employee benefit) trust, investment trust, and custodial.

GASB. The Governmental Accounting Standards Board (GASB), organized in 1984 by the Financial Accounting Foundation (FAF) to establish standards of financial accounting and reporting for state and local governmental entities. Its standards guide the preparation of external financial reports of those entities.

general fund. The fund within the governmental category used to account for all financial resources, except those required to be accounted for in another governmental fund.

general-purpose governments. Governmental entities that provide a range of services, such as states, cities, counties, towns, and villages.

governmental funds. Funds used to account for the acquisition, use, and balances of spendable financial resources and the related current liabilities, except those accounted for in proprietary funds and fiduciary funds. Essentially, these funds are accounting segregations of financial resources. Spendable assets are assigned to a particular government fund type according to the purposes for which they may or must be used. Current liabilities are assigned to the fund type from which they are to be paid. The difference between the assets and liabilities of governmental fund types is referred to as *fund balance*. The measurement focus in these fund types is on the determination of financial position and changes in financial position (sources, uses, and balances of financial resources), rather than on net income determination.

government-wide financial statements. Highly aggregated financial statements that present financial information for all assets (including infrastructure capital assets), liabilities, and net assets of a primary government and its component units, except for fiduciary funds. The government-wide financial statements use the economic resources measurement focus and accrual basis of accounting.

infrastructure assets. Long-lived capital assets that normally are stationary in nature and can be preserved for a significantly greater number of years than most capital assets. Examples of infrastructure assets are roads, bridges, tunnels, drainage systems, water and sewer systems, dams, and lighting systems. Buildings, except those that are an ancillary part of a network of infrastructure assets, are not considered infrastructure assets.

interfund receivable/payable. Activity between funds of a government reflecting amounts provided with a requirement for repayment, or sales and purchases of goods and services between funds approximating their external exchange value (also referred to as **interfund loans** or **interfund services provided and used**).

internal service fund. A generic fund type within the proprietary category used to account for the financing of goods or services provided by one department or agency to other departments or agencies of a government, or to other governments, on a cost-reimbursement basis.

investment trust fund. A generic fund type within the fiduciary category used by a government in a fiduciary capacity, such as to maintain its cash and investment pool for other governments.

major funds. A government's general fund (or its equivalent), other individual governmental type, and enterprise funds that meet specific quantitative criteria, and any other governmental or enterprise fund that a government's officials believe is particularly important to financial statement users.

management's discussion and analysis. Management's discussion and analysis, or MD&A, is required supplementary information that introduces the basic financial statements by presenting certain financial information as well as management's analytical insights on that information.

measurement focus. The accounting convention that determines (*a*) which assets and which liabilities are included on a government's balance sheet and where they are reported, and (*b*) whether an operating statement presents information on the flow of financial resources (revenues and expenditures) or information on the flow of economic resources (revenues and expenses).

modified accrual basis of accounting. The basis of accounting adapted to the governmental fund type measurement focus. Revenues and other financial resource increments are recognized when they become both *measurable* and *available to finance expenditures of the current period*. *Available* means collectible in the current period or soon enough thereafter to be used to pay liabilities of the current period. Expenditures are recognized when the fund liability is incurred and expected to be paid from current resources, except for (*a*) inventories of materials and supplies that may be considered expenditures either when purchased or when used, and (*b*) prepaid insurance and similar items that may be considered expenditures either when paid for or when consumed. All governmental funds are accounted for using the modified accrual basis of accounting in fund financial statements.

modified approach. Rules that allow infrastructure assets that are part of a network or subsystem of a network not to be depreciated as long as certain requirements are met.

net position. The residual of all other elements presented in a statement of financial position.

nonspendable fund balance. The portion of fund balance that includes amounts that cannot be spent because they are either (*a*) not in spendable form or (*b*) legally or contractually required to be maintained intact.

pension (and other employee benefit) trust fund. A trust fund used to account for a public employees retirement system, OPEB plan, or other employee benefits other than pensions that are administered through trusts that meet specified criteria. Pension (and other employee benefit) trust funds use the accrual basis of accounting and the flow of economic resources measurement focus.

permanent fund. A generic fund type under the governmental category used to report resources that are legally restricted to the extent that only earnings, and not principal, may be used for purposes that support the reporting government's programs and, therefore, are for the benefit of the government or its citizenry. (Permanent funds do not include private-purpose trust funds, which should be used when the government is required to use the principal or earnings for the benefit of individuals, private organizations, or other governments).

private purpose trust fund. A general fund type under the fiduciary category used to report resources held and administered by the reporting government acting in a fiduciary capacity for individuals, other governments, or private organizations.

proprietary funds. The government category used to account for a government's ongoing organizations and activities that are similar to those often found in the private sector (these are enterprise and internal service funds). All assets, liabilities, equities, revenues, expenses, and transfers relating to the government's business and quasi-business activities are accounted for through proprietary funds. Proprietary funds should apply all applicable GASB pronouncements and those GAAP applicable to similar businesses in the private sector, unless those conflict with GASB pronouncements. These funds use the accrual basis of accounting in conjunction with the flow of economic resources measurement focus.

purchases method. The method under which inventories are recorded as expenditures when acquired.

restricted fund balance. Portion of fund balance that reflects constraints placed on the use of resources (other than nonspendable items) that are either (a) externally imposed by a creditor, such as through debt covenants, grantors, contributors, or laws or regulations of other governments or (b) imposed by law through constitutional provisions or enabling legislation.

required supplementary information. GAAP specify that certain information be presented as required supplementary information, or RSI.

special-purpose governments. Legally separate entities that perform only one activity or a few activities, such as cemetery districts, school districts, colleges and universities, utilities, hospitals and other health care organizations, and public employee retirement systems.

special revenue fund. A fund that must have revenue or proceeds from specific revenue sources that are either restricted or committed for a specific purpose other than debt service or capital projects. This definition means that in order to be considered a special revenue fund, there must be one or more revenue sources upon which reporting the activity in a separate fund is predicated.

interfund transfers. All transfers, such as legally authorized transfers from a fund receiving revenue to a fund through which the resources are to be expended, where there is no intent to repay. Interfund transfers are recorded on the operating statement.

unassigned fund balance. Residual classification for the general fund. This classification represents fund balance that has not been assigned to other funds and has not been restricted, committed, or assigned to specific purposes within the general fund. The general fund should be the only fund that reports a positive unassigned fund balance amount. In other funds, if expenditures incurred for specific purposes exceeded the amounts restricted, committed, or assigned to those purposes, it may be necessary to report a negative unassigned fund balance.

unrestricted fund balance. The total of committed fund balance, assigned fund balance, and unassigned fund balance.

Not-for-profit terminology

board-designated endowment fund. An endowment fund created by a not-for-profit entity's governing board by designating a portion of its net assets without donor restrictions to be invested to provide income for a long, but not necessarily specified, period. In rare circumstances, a board-designated endowment fund also can include a portion of net assets with donor restrictions. For example, if a not-for-profit is unable to spend donor-restricted contributions in the near term, then the board sometimes considers the long-term investment of these funds.

board-designated net assets. Net assets without donor restrictions subject to self-imposed limits by action of the governing board. Board-designated net assets may be earmarked for future programs, investment, contingencies, purchase or construction of fixed assets, or other uses. Some governing boards may delegate designation decisions to internal management. Such designations are considered to be included in board-designated net assets.

charitable lead trust. A trust established in connection with a split-interest agreement in which the not-for-profit entity receives distributions during the agreement's term. Upon termination of the trust, the remainder of the trust assets are paid to the donor or to third-party beneficiaries designated by the donor.

charitable remainder trust. A trust established in connection with a split-interest agreement in which the donor or a third-party beneficiary receives specified distributions during the agreement's term. Upon termination of the trust, a not-for-profit entity receives the assets remaining in the trust.

collections. Works of art, historical treasures, or similar assets that are (*a*) held for public exhibition, education, or research in furtherance of public service, rather than financial gain; (*b*) protected, kept unencumbered, cared for, and preserved; and (*c*) subject to an organizational policy that requires the proceeds of items that are sold to be used to acquire other items for collections.

conditional promise to give. A promise to give that is subject to a donor-imposed condition.

contribution. An unconditional transfer of cash or other assets, as well as unconditional promises to give, to an entity or a reduction, settlement, or cancellation of its liabilities in a voluntary nonreciprocal transfer by another entity acting other than as an owner.

costs of joint activities. Costs incurred for a joint activity. Costs of joint activities may include joint costs and costs other than joint costs. *Costs other than joint costs* are costs that are identifiable with a particular function, such as program, fund-raising, management and general, and membership development costs.

donor-imposed restriction. A donor stipulation (*donors* include other types of contributors, including makers of certain grants) that specifies a use for the contributed asset that is more specific than broad limits resulting from the nature of the organization, the environment in which it operates, and the purposes specified in its articles of incorporation or bylaws, or comparable documents for an unincorporated association. A restriction on an organization's use of the asset contributed may be temporary in nature or perpetual in nature.

donor-restricted endowment fund. An endowment fund that is created by a donor stipulation (*donors* include other types of contributors, including makers of certain grants) that requires investment of the gift in perpetuity or for a specified term. Some donors or laws may require that a portion of income, gains, or both be added to the gift and invested subject to similar restrictions.

donor-restricted support. Donor-restricted revenues or gains from contributions that increase net assets with donor restrictions (*donors* include other types of contributions, including makers of certain grants).

economic interest. A not-for-profit entity's interest in another entity that exists if any of the following criteria are met: (*a*) The other entity holds or uses significant resources that must be used for the purposes of the not-for-profit entity, either directly or indirectly, by producing income or providing services, or (*b*) the not-for-profit entity is responsible for the liabilities of the other entity.

endowment fund. An established fund of cash, securities, or other assets that provides income for the maintenance of a not-for-profit entity. The use of the assets of the fund may be with or without donor-imposed restrictions. Endowment funds generally are established by donor-restricted gifts and bequests to provide a source of income.

functional expense classification. A method of grouping expenses according to the purpose for which the costs are incurred. The primary functional classifications of a not-for-profit entity are program services and supporting activities.

funds functioning as endowment. Net assets without donor restrictions (*donors* include other types of contributors, including makers of certain grants) designated by an entity's governing board to be invested to provide income for generally a long, but not necessarily specified, period.

joint activity. An activity that is part of the fund-raising function and has elements of one or more other functions, such as programs, management and general, membership development, or any other functional category used by the entity.

joint costs. The costs of conducting joint activities that are not identifiable with a particular component of the activity.

management and general activities. Supporting activities that are not directly identifiable with one or more programs, fund-raising activities, or membership development activities.

natural expense classification. A method of grouping expenses according to the kinds of economic benefits received in incurring those expenses. Examples of natural expense classifications include salaries and wages, employee benefits, professional services, supplies, interest expense, rent, utilities, and depreciation.

net assets. The excess or deficiency of assets over liabilities of a not-for-profit entity, which is divided into two mutually exclusive classes according to the existence or absence of donor-imposed restrictions.

net assets with donor restrictions. The part of net assets of a not-for-profit entity that is subject to donor-imposed restrictions (*donors* include other types of contributors, including makers of certain grants).

net assets without donor restrictions. The part of net assets of a not-for-profit entity that is not subject to donor-imposed restrictions (*donors* include other types of contributors, including makers of certain grants).

programmatic investing. The activity of making loans or other investments that are directed at carrying out a not-for-profit entity's purpose for existence, rather than investing in the general production of income or appreciation of an asset (for example, total return investing). An example of programmatic investing is a loan made to lower-income individuals to promote home ownership.

promise to give. A written or oral agreement to contribute cash or other assets to another entity. A promise to give may be either conditional or unconditional.

underwater endowment fund. A donor-restricted endowment fund for which the fair value of the fund at the reporting date is less than either the original gift amount or the amount required to be maintained by the donor or by law that extends donor restrictions.

Single audit and Yellow Book terminology

attestation engagements. Attestation engagements concern examining, reviewing, or performing agreed-upon procedures on a subject matter or an assertion about a subject matter and reporting on the results.

compliance supplement. A document issued annually in the spring by the OMB to provide guidance to auditors.

data collection form. A form submitted to the Federal Audit Clearinghouse that provides information about the auditor, the auditee and its federal programs, and the results of the audit.

federal financial assistance. Assistance that nonfederal entities receive or administer in the form of grants, loans, loan guarantees, property, cooperative agreements, interest subsidies, insurance, food commodities, direct appropriations, or other assistance, but does not include amounts received as reimbursement for services rendered to individuals in accordance with guidance issued by the director.

financial audits. Financial audits are primarily concerned with providing reasonable assurance about whether financial statements are presented fairly, in all material respects, in conformity with GAAP or with a comprehensive basis of accounting other than GAAP.

GAGAS. Generally accepted government auditing standards issued by the GAO. They are published as *Government Auditing Standards*, also commonly known as the Yellow Book.

GAO. The United States Government Accountability Office. Among its responsibilities is the issuance of GAGAS.

OMB. The Office of Management and Budget. The OMB assists the President in the development and implementation of budget, program, management, and regulatory policies.

pass-through entity. A nonfederal entity that provides federal awards to a subrecipient to carry out a federal program.

performance audits. Performance audits entail an objective and systematic examination of evidence to provide an independent assessment of the performance and management of a program against objective criteria as well as assessments that provide a prospective focus or that synthesize information on best practices or cross-cutting issues.

program-specific audit. A compliance audit of one federal program.

single audit. An audit of a nonfederal entity that includes the entity's financial statements and federal awards.

single audit guide. This AICPA Audit Guide, formally titled Government Auditing Standards *and Single Audits*, is the former Statement of Position (SOP) 98-3, *Audits of States, Local Governments, and Not-for-Profit Organizations Receiving Federal Awards*. The single audit guide provides guidance on the auditor's responsibilities when conducting a single audit or program-specific audit in accordance with the Single Audit Act, GAGAS, and the Uniform Guidance.

subrecipient. A nonfederal entity that receives federal awards through another nonfederal entity to carry out a federal program but does not include an individual who receives financial assistance through such awards.

Uniform Guidance. Formally known as Title 2 U.S. *Code of Federal Regulations* Part 200, *Uniform Administrative Requirements, Cost Principles, and Audit Requirements for Federal Awards*. The Uniform Guidance sets forth the requirements for the compliance audit portion of a single audit.

Index

The New Yellow Book: Government Auditing Standards, 2018 Version

By Rebecca A. Meyer, CPA, CGMA

Solutions

The AICPA publishes *CPA Letter Daily*, a free e-newsletter published each weekday. The newsletter, which covers the 10-12 most important stories in business, finance, and accounting, as well as AICPA information, was created to deliver news to CPAs and others who work with the accounting profession. Besides summarizing media articles, commentaries, and research results, the e-newsletter links to television broadcasts and videos and features reader polls. *CPA Letter Daily*'s editors scan hundreds of publications and websites, selecting the most relevant and important news so you don't have to. The newsletter arrives in your inbox early in the morning. To sign up, visit smartbrief.com/CPA.

Do you need high-quality technical assistance? The AICPA Auditing and Accounting Technical Hotline provides non-authoritative guidance on accounting, auditing, attestation, and compilation and review standards. The hotline can be reached at 877.242.7212.

Solutions

Chapter 1

Knowledge check solutions

1.
    a. Incorrect. GAGAS may apply due to contractual requirements.

    b. Incorrect. A GAGAS audit may be required due to regulatory requirements.

    c. Incorrect. A GAGAS audit may be performed voluntarily.

    d. Correct. GAAS has no provisions that would require a GAGAS audit.

2.
    a. Correct. An actuary engaged by an audit team to assist in the performance of an engagement subject to GAGAS does not meet the definition of an auditor under GAGAS.

    b. Incorrect. An engagement partner responsible for planning a performance audit conducted in accordance with GAGAS meets the definition of auditor.

    c. Incorrect. A federal internal inspector who reports on investigations related to the programs and operations of the federal agency meets the definition of auditor.

    d. Incorrect. A staff person performing agreed-upon procedures over a contract that is required to be conducted in accordance with the Yellow Book meets the definition of an auditor.

Chapter 2

Knowledge check solutions

1.
    a. Incorrect. Application guidance is not indicated by font color.

    b. Correct. Application guidance may contain various pieces of information regarding requirements, including further explanation of the requirement.

    c. Incorrect. GAGAS states that the auditor should understand both the requirements and application guidance in order to understand the intent of a requirements and to apply the requirement properly.

    d. Incorrect. Application guidance is found immediately after the related requirement.

2.
- a. Incorrect. The Yellow Book does not require that auditors follow the Uniform Guidance.
- b. Incorrect. GAGAS is required to be followed in a Uniform Guidance compliance audit.
- c. Incorrect. GAAS does not require the use of GAGAS in any type of engagement.
- d. Correct. GAGAS is required to be followed in a Uniform Guidance compliance audit.

Chapter 3

Case 3-1 suggested solution

Summary of issue in situation 1

Examples of circumstances that create self-interest threats for an auditor include

> a member of the audit team entering into employment negotiations with an audited entity.

If Peter is approached by the client and says "No, thank you," then all he would have to do is tell the partner that a position was discussed and he declined the offer. However, if Peter tells the client that he will think about it, or asks for further details, then Peter has started to enter the realm of a self-interest threat. He needs to inform the partner of the discussions and request that he be removed from the engagement team until the decision is made. However, if Peter starts to negotiate salary and conditions of employment (such as vacation, sick time, and so on), then he should inform the partner and they should remove him from any contact with the engagement team until such negotiations collapse or he leaves and is employed by the client. We suggest participants not get hung up on the phrase "entering into employment negotiations" and look at the nuances of this case. The GAO has indicated through discussions of this case that there would be an appearance threat if he does not say "No" to the offer.

Peter needs to make a decision on whether he would like to move toward being considered for the formal offer. If the position has been offered and Peter has not declined, he would have a self-interest threat and should be disassociated with the audit until he declines, the offer is withdrawn, or another individual is selected for the position. In other words, until he declines, Peter would be considered to be in employment negotiations.

Summary of issue in situation 2

Examples of circumstances that create self-review threats for an auditor include

> A member of the audit team being, or having recently been, employed by the audited entity in a position to exert significant influence over the subject matter of the audit.

Because John worked in the position that affected the accounting records and other data that are the subject matter of audit this year, he should be reassigned and not permitted to work on the audit this year. The firm may consider his inclusion on the next year's audit provided there are no other threats identified at that time.

Summary of issue in situation 3

Examples of circumstances that create bias threats for an auditor include

> an auditor's having biases associated with political, ideological, or social convictions that result from membership or employment in, or loyalty to, a particular type of policy, group, organization, or level of government that could affect the auditor's objectivity.

Because Tom is only a staff person, his political activity would probably not affect the firm's ability to do the audits of the governmental clients. If he were of a higher position within the firm, such as a partner, or maybe a manager, then there would be an appearance problem due to the potential loyalty issues. Tom may need to rethink his political activity as he progresses with the firm.

Summary of issue in situation 4

Examples of circumstances that create familiarity threats for an auditor include

> senior audit personnel having a long association with the audited entity.

The firm may need to rethink Francine's involvement with the client. The appearance issue is an item to consider. Annette Summer, the quality control partner, may be used as a safeguard by having her review the working papers in more detail. If the client does not object, a change of in-charge partner may be the best solution. This does become a troubling issue with the longevity of the firm and a lack of internal policy of rotating the in-charge partner every five years or more.

Summary of issue in situation 5

Examples of circumstances that create undue influence threats for an auditor or audit organization include existence of

> unreasonable restrictions on the time allowed to complete an audit or issue the report.

In addition to this being a threat to independence under the Yellow Book, it is also a fraud issue under the auditing standards. The firm must identify the true reason for the request to cut the audit time by five weeks through further inquiry of other individuals, including board members. This threat could be eliminated (provided there is a true reason for shortening the time) by assigning more staff or bringing in some per diem CPAs to assist in the audit process. Extensive supervision by highly qualified staff is essential.

Summary of issue in situation 6

Examples of circumstances that create management participation threats for an auditor include

> an audit organization principal or employee serving as a voting member of an entity's management committee or board of directors, making policy decisions that affect future direction and operation of an entity's programs, supervising entity employees, developing or approving programmatic policy, authorizing an entity's transactions, or maintaining custody of an entity's assets.

The partners should object to Maggie becoming a trustee. Being a voting member of the client would definitely violate the Yellow Book and the AICPA's independence rules. Jennifer Kapplinger, however, could serve on the ad hoc committee, provided that the committee will only make recommendations and the final decisions will be made at the board level. She probably should not chair the committee.

Summary of issue in situation 7

Examples of circumstances that create self-interest threats for an auditor include

> an audit organization having undue dependence on income from a particular audited entity.

This will be a situation to which some participants will not see a problem, although others may find it questionable. The percentage of income requires professional judgment because there are no set guidelines found in authoritative literature. It is the author's opinion that if the firm could survive the removal of the client and be able to restructure the firm through staff lay-offs, with no change to partners' status, then there may be no threat. However, the firm should document the threat and document why they believe that this threat does not taint their professional judgment or independence in the audit process. The firm should also consider periodically rotating the partner and audit team to add a safeguard to avoid any appearance issues by a knowledgeable third party.

Solution to case study 3-2

Nonaudit service provided by Audit Organization ABC	Effect on independence
Hiring or terminating the audited entity's employees	**Impairment**
Preparing financial statements in their entirety from a client-provided trial balance	Significant threat
Evaluation of an entity's system of internal control performed outside the audit	Threat
Approving entity transactions	Impairment
Supervising ongoing monitoring procedures over an entity's system of internal control	Impairment
Preparing certain line items or sections of the financial statements based on information in the trial balance	Threat
Preparing account reconciliations that identify reconciling items for the audited entity management's evaluation	Threat
Changing journal entries without management approval	Impairment
Posting coded transactions to an audited entity's general ledger	Threat
Educating the audited entity about matters that are readily available to the auditors, such as best practices or benchmarking studies	No threat (routine activity)
Making changes to source documents without management's approval	Impairment

Knowledge check solutions

1.
    a. Incorrect. The ethical principle described is not the public interest.

    b. Correct. Objectivity, which includes being independent of mind and appearance, is the ethical principle described.

    c. Incorrect. The ethical principle described is not professional behavior.

    d. Incorrect. The ethical principle described is not proper use of government information, resources, and position.

2.
    a. Incorrect. A bias threat is a category of threat in GAGAS.

    b. Correct. Documentation is not a category of threat per GAGAS.

    c. Incorrect. An undue influence threat is a category of threat in GAGAS.

    d. Incorrect. A structural threat is a category of threat in GAGAS.

3.
    a. Incorrect. The description given is not a management participation threat.

    b. Incorrect. The description given is not a structural threat.

    c. Incorrect. The description given is not a bias threat.

    d. Correct. The description given is an undue influence threat.

4.
    a. Correct. Documentation of the understanding with the audited entity is not part of the conceptual framework.

    b. Incorrect. The application of safeguards is part of the conceptual framework.

    c. Incorrect. Identifying threats is part of the conceptual framework.

    d. Incorrect. Evaluating the significance of threats is part of the conceptual framework.

5.
    a. Incorrect. Not including individuals who performed the nonaudit service as engagement team members is an example of a safeguard.

    b. Incorrect. Having another audit organization evaluate the results of the nonaudit service is an example of a safeguard.

    c. Incorrect. Having a professional staff member not involved with the nonaudit service review the engagement and nonaudit work performed is an example of a safeguard.

    d. Correct. Not removing this individual in a timely manner could cause a threat to independence.

6.

 a. Incorrect. Deciding which recommendations of the auditor or third party to implement is considered a management responsibility.

 b. Correct. Providing advice to the audited entity on routine business matters is not considered a management responsibility.

 c. Incorrect. Having custody of the audited entity assets is considered a management responsibility.

 d. Incorrect. Setting policies and strategic direction for the audited entity is considered a management responsibility.

Chapter 4

Solution to exercise 4-1

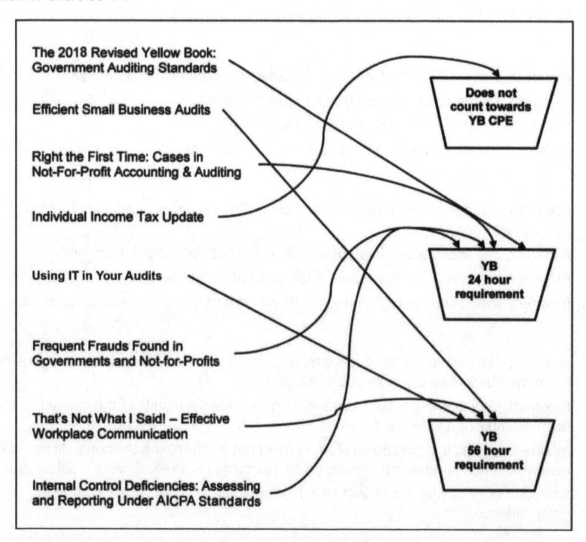

Case study 4-1 suggested solution

Bill Viper, manager					
Course title	Hours earned in 20X1	Hours earned in 20X2	Qualifies for the YB 24 hours	Qualifies for the YB 56 hours	Does not qualify for YB
Advanced Auditing of HHS Block Grants	8		8		
Individual Tax Update	8				8
Financial and Tax Planning for High-Income Clients	8				8
Recent Developments in Estate Planning	8				8
The AICPA Guide to Consolidations, Business Combinations, and Combined Financial Statements	8			8	
Auditing Student Financial Aid		8	8		
Innovative Tax Planning for Individuals and Sole Proprietors		8			8
Not-for-Profit Auditing: Auditing Financial Results		8	8		
Compilations and Reviews of Financial Statements		8		8	
Retirement Tax Planning that Works for Your Clients		8			8
Total qualifying for the YB 24 hours			24		
Total qualifying for the YB 56 hours				16	

Did Bill meet the CPE requirements? No. Because it appears that none of the taxation courses taken likely relate to an objective or the subject matter of an audit, training in those related topics would not qualify as CPE under generally accepted government auditing standards (GAGAS). This leaves Bill far short of meeting the 56-hour component.

Irene Bentley, senior					
Course title	Hours earned in 20X1	Hours earned in 20X2	Qualifies for the YB 24 hours	Qualifies for the YB 56 hours	Does not qualify for YB
AICPA Form 990 Not-for-Profit Workshop[1]	8		8		
Not-for-Profit Auditing: Auditing Financial Results	8		8		
Becoming a 1040 Hero	8				8
Recent Developments in Estate Planning	8				8
Financial and Tax Planning for High-Income Clients	8				8
Auditing Student Financial Aid		8	8		
Construction Contractors: Accounting and Auditing		8		8	
Not-for-Profit Accounting and Auditing Update Conference		16	16		
Forensic Auditing: Fraudulent Reporting and Concealed Assets		8		8	
Studies on Single Audit and Yellow Book Deficiencies		8	8		
Audits of Small Businesses		8		8	
Solving Complex Single Audit Issues for Government and Not-for-Profit Organizations		8	8		
Total qualifying for the YB 24 hours			56		
Total qualifying for the YB 56 hours				24	

Did Irene meet the CPE requirements? No. This one is a little tough. Irene has taken 80 hours that would qualify and was heavy in the courses that would count for the 24 hours. However, at least 20 hours of the 80 should be completed in any one year of the two-year period. In year 20X1 she only obtained 16 hours that would qualify toward the 80.

---

[1] Assume knowledge of the relevant tax requirements relates to an important financial reporting objective that influences reporting for purposes of the financial statements, such as categorization of expenses, prohibited transactions, or unrelated business taxable income.

	Sandy Dodge, staff				
Course title	Hours earned in 20X1	Hours earned in 20X2	Qualifies for the YB 24 hours	Qualifies for the YB 56 hours	Does not qualify for YB
Effective Internal Controls for Small Businesses	8			8	
Federal Tax Update for Individuals	8				8
Cost Allocation Methods for Not-for-Profit Organizations	8		8		
Form 5500: Prepare it Fast – File it Right...The 1st Time[2]	8			8	
Reporting and Disclosure Problems for Small Businesses	8			8	
Using the AICPA Not-for-Profit Entities Audit and Accounting Guide	8		8		
Fraud and the Financial Statement Audit: Auditor Responsibilities Under AU-C section 240		8	8		
Innovative Tax Planning for Individuals		8			8
Audit Staff Training: Level III		24		24	
Audits of Small Businesses		8		8	
Total qualifying for the YB 24 hours			24		
Total qualifying for the YB 56 hours				56	

Did Sandy meet the CPE requirements? Yes. Some may question whether fraud course would qualify for the 24 hours. Because the SASs are incorporated by reference in the Yellow Book, courses on the AICPA standards for performing audits and the related audit reporting would count toward the 24 hours (as would applicable courses on the AICPA SSAE). For the entire 8 hours to count toward the 24-hour requirement, the course needs to be focused on specific GAAS guidance and not a more generic audit course that covers issues other than the guidance at length (to the degree that generic audit topics other than the AU-C sections are discussed the hours would have to be allocated between the 24 hour and 56 hour requirements).

---

[2] Assume the taxation or other topics in the course relate to an objective or subject matter of an audit engagement Sandy works on.

Course title	Hours earned in 20X1	Hours earned in 20X2	Qualifies for the YB 24 hours	Qualifies for the YB 56 hours	Does not qualify for YB
Audits of Small Businesses	8			8	
Payroll Taxes and 1099s: Everything You Need to Know	16				16
Employee Benefit Plans: Audit and Accounting Essentials	8			8	
Cash Flow Statement: Preparation, Presentation, and Use	8			8	
Audit Staff Training Level 1		24		24	
Federal Tax Update for Individuals		8			8
Audits of Construction Contractors		8		8	
Total qualifying for the YB 24 hours			0		
Total qualifying for the YB 56 hours				56	

Tom Sedan, staff assistant

Did Tom meet the CPE requirements? No. Because Tom is only involved in performing audit procedures but not involved in planning, directing, or reporting on the audit or attestation engagements, and he charges less than 20% of his time annually to audits and attestations conducted in accordance with the Yellow Book, he should comply with the 24-hour requirement and is exempt from the 56-hour requirement. In this case, he complied with the 56 but not the 24.

Knowledge check solutions

1.

   a. Incorrect. GAGAS requirements and guidance related to competence do not include audited entity staff.

   b. Correct. Nonsupervisory auditors, specialists, and partners and directors are included in the GAGAS requirements and guidance related to competence.

   c. Incorrect. GAGAS requirements and guidance related to competence do not apply to support staff.

   d. Incorrect. GAGAS requirements and guidance related to competence do not apply to audited entity finance office staff.

2.

    a. Incorrect. Supervisory roles are considered to have work situations characterized by a moderate level of ambiguity, complexity, and uncertainty.

    b. Incorrect. Nonsupervisory roles are considered to have work situations characterized by a low level of ambiguity, complexity, and uncertainty.

    c. Incorrect. Specialists are not described in these terms.

    d. Correct. Partners and directors are considered to have work situations characterized by a high level of ambiguity, complexity, and uncertainty.

3.

    a. Incorrect. Every 2 years, at least 24 hours of CPE that directly relates to the government environment, government auditing, or the specific or unique environment in which the audited entity operates should be obtained by auditors who plan engagement procedures in a GAGAS audit.

    b. Incorrect. Auditors described here are required to obtain the stated CPE.

    c. Correct. Auditors that are required to take the total 80 hours of CPE under GAGAS are required to complete at least 20 (not 24) hours of CPE in each year of the 2-year period.

    d. Incorrect. There is a provision that auditors hired or initially assigned to GAGAS audits after the beginning of an audit organization's 2-year CPE period may complete a prorated number of CPE hours.

Chapter 5

Knowledge check solutions

1.

    a. Incorrect. Policies and procedures related to personnel evaluations are required under the Human Resources component of the quality control system.

    b. Incorrect. Policies and procedures to ensure that the audit organization only undertakes engagements if it has the time and resources to do so under are required under the Initiation, Acceptance, and Continuance of audits component of the quality control system.

    c. Correct. Policies and procedures on when and how to consult on complicated matters is required under the engagement performance component of the quality control system.

    d. Incorrect. Policies to ensure that those assigned responsibility for the system of quality control have the authority to assume that responsibility are required under the leadership responsibilities for quality within the organization component of the quality control system.

2.

    a. Correct. The date the monitoring procedures were performed is not required to be communicated.

    b. Incorrect. The communication should include, when relevant, a description of systemic, repetitive, or other deficiencies and of the actions taken to resolve those deficiencies.

    c. Incorrect. The conclusions reached from the monitoring procedures is required.

    d. Incorrect. A description of monitoring procedures performed is required.

3.

    a. Incorrect. An external peer review is required at least once every three years.

    b. Incorrect. There are no special provisions in the event of no deficiencies being found.

    c. Incorrect. A client requesting a peer review report is not what determines the requirement for obtaining a peer review.

    d. Correct. Audit organizations performing GAGAS engagements are required to obtain an external peer review at least once every three years.

4.

    a. Incorrect. Fail with deficiencies is not a type of peer review report.

    b. Correct. Pass, pass with deficiencies, and fail are all types of peer review reports.

    c. Incorrect. Unmodified, qualified, adverse, and disclaimer are not types of peer review reports.

    d. Incorrect. Disclaimer is not a type of peer review report.

Chapter 6

Solution to exercise 6-1

Cause	1. City officials explained that they were familiar with other grant programs where in-kind payments qualified as grant expenditures. They avowed not having read the fine print requirement for Urban Development Action Grant (UDAG) matching payments to be in cash and only for direct costs. The city officials who signed the grant said the matching requirement was not set forth in the documents they signed but acknowledged that it may have been in 20 or so pages of boilerplate attached to the documents.

Condition	2. The city reported final project costs at $830,000 and city expenditures at $190,000. Review of the city records showed that of the $190,000,
	    a. $110,000 was for land and rights-of-way the city already owned;
	    b. $60,200 was for all allocated salaries of city staff administering grant construction work that was done on contract; and
	    c. $19,800 was for meters and valves the city purchased for the project and provided to the contractor.

Effect	3.	The city is required by grant terms to expend $160,000 in matching payments on grant costs. Of the city's reported grant expenditures, only $19,800 qualifies as a matching payment. The difference of $140,200 qualifies as a liability, and this amount is considered material relative to the financial statements.
Condition	4.	The city of Zahl was awarded UDAG funding of $800,000 to extend its water and sewer system to a small industrial park. This improvement grant was awarded to attract a wholesale distribution firm that would develop the park and employ up to 100 people. Zahl is located at an intersection of three interstate highways.
Criteria	5.	Recipients of UDAG funding are required by law to pay 20% of the amount of the awarded grant. This matching 20% must be in cash and expended on direct costs of the project.
Condition	6.	Zahl is a small city by UDAG criteria, and it meets UDAG criteria as a "distressed" area. The city lost two small manufacturing plants in the past year with a combined employment of 125 people.

Solution to case study 6-1

There are many ways to write up a finding. Although your descriptions of the elements may be different from the descriptions noted here, you can see if you captured the essential elements of the finding elements and possible auditor recommendation. Although the auditor does not draft the management response, this is a response that management might provide to the auditor.

Criteria	1.	Management of the entity is responsible for complying with laws and regulations. This responsibility includes establishing the necessary internal controls to ensure such compliance.
Condition	2.	The entity was provided $100 million to carry out its programs. Program legislation and regulations imposed several requirements on the use of the funds. The entity has not established internal controls to ensure compliance with these requirements.
Effect	3.	Substantive audit tests for compliance with the requirements applicable to use of the funds did not reveal instances of noncompliance material to the financial statements. However, due to its significance, we consider this condition to be a material weakness in internal controls.
Cause	4.	The entity's management had not undertaken the necessary steps to establish appropriate internal controls to help ensure compliance with laws and regulations.
Recommendation	5.	We recommend that the entity officials expedite the establishment and maintenance of the appropriate internal controls to provide reasonable assurance of compliance with laws and regulations.
Management Response	6.	The entity's officials promised that they would establish and maintain internal controls that would help ensure compliance with appropriate laws and regulations.

Knowledge check solutions

1.

    a. Incorrect. The stated purpose is not to determine if the auditor should accept the engagement.

    b. Incorrect. Information received regarding previous audits and attestation engagements is not used to determine if the auditor should issue an unmodified opinion on the financial statements.

    c. Incorrect. The stated purpose is not to evaluate the honesty of audited entity officials.

    d. Correct. The stated purpose of this requirement is to evaluate if the audited entity has taken appropriate corrective action to address significant findings and recommendations from the previous engagement.

2.

    a. Correct. All persons performing the engagement should be a licensed CPA, licensed accountant, or a person working for a licensed CPA firm.

    b. Incorrect. GAGAS does not require this when working for a government audit organization.

    c. Incorrect. This is not one of the requirements when working on a financial audit of an entity operating outside the U.S.

    d. Incorrect. The standard does not have the same requirements for a government audit organization as it has for CPA firms.

3.

    a. Incorrect. A purpose of this element is to provide context for evaluating evidence and understanding the finding.

    b. Correct. Poorly designed policies and procedures would not be a criterion but could be a cause.

    c. Incorrect. Expected performance may be one criterion.

    d. Incorrect. Laws and regulations may be one criterion.

4.

    a. Incorrect. Auditors should plan and perform procedures to develop the elements of a finding.

    b. Incorrect. GAGAS states that internal control deficiencies should be a consideration when developing the cause element of a finding.

    c. Correct. Auditors may consider whether and how to communicate instances of waste and abuse if they become aware of them.

    d. Incorrect. This is an auditor consideration as it relates to the element of effect or potential effect.

5.
   a. Incorrect. Placing perspective in the elements of a finding assists readers in judging the prevalence and potential consequences of the finding.
   b. Incorrect. The nature and cause are part of presenting findings.
   c. Correct. Auditors may provide recommendations for corrective action but are not required to.
   d. Incorrect. The elements of a finding should assist management and oversight officials in understanding the need for corrective action.

6.
   a. Correct. If it is determined that omitted material could distort the audit results or conceal improper or illegal practices, the audit report language should be revised to avoid report users from drawing inappropriate conclusions.
   b. Incorrect. If information is prohibited from public disclosure, auditors should disclose that certain information has been omitted and the circumstances that make the omission necessary.
   c. Incorrect. Auditors may issue a separate, classified, or limited use report containing omitted information and distribute the report only to persons authorized by law or regulation to receive it.
   d. Incorrect. The reference to the omitted information in auditor reporting may be general and not specific.

Chapter 7

Knowledge check solutions

1.
   a. Incorrect. Auditors are required to comply with both GAGAS and AICPA standards when conducting attestation engagements under GAGAS.
   b. Incorrect. Auditors are required to comply with both GAGAS and AICPA standards when conducting attestation engagements under GAGAS.
   c. Incorrect. Auditors are required to comply with both GAGAS and AICPA standards when conducting attestation engagements under GAGAS.
   d. Correct. Auditors performing GAGAS attestation engagements should comply with both GAGAS and AICPA standards when citing GAGAS in all types of attestation reports.

2.

   a. Incorrect. Additional GAGAS requirements related to reporting deficiencies in internal control are applicable only to the examination type of attestation engagement.

   b. Incorrect. Additional GAGAS requirements related to reporting the auditor's compliance with GAGAS is applicable for all types of attestation engagements and reviews of financial statements under GAGAS.

   c. Correct. Additional GAGAS requirements related to reporting findings directly to outside parties is applicable only to the examination type of attestation engagement.

   d. Incorrect. Additional GAGAS requirements related to findings is applicable only to the examination type of attestation engagement.

3.

   a. Incorrect. Working for a U.S. licensed certified public accounting firm is one, but not the only, requirement that would permit an auditor to perform the engagement.

   b. Correct. Auditors should include all the required reporting elements related to agreed-upon procedures contained in the SSAEs when citing GAGAS in their agreed-upon procedures reports .

   c. Incorrect. Requirements concerning the consideration of noncompliance with laws and regulations should be extended to also include noncompliance with provisions of contracts and grant agreements in the agreed-upon procedures engagement under GAGAS.

   d. Incorrect. The additional GAGAS requirement related to findings is not applicable in an agreed-upon procedures engagement under GAGAS.

Chapter 8

Knowledge check solutions

1.

   a. Correct. GAGAS does not require the auditor to plan the audit to obtain a low level of control risk but states that the auditor should plan the performance audit to reduce audit risk to an acceptably low level. It is not required that a low level of audit risk be achieved.

   b. Incorrect. Planning the performance audit should aim to reduce audit risk to an acceptably low level.

   c. Incorrect. Planning the performance audit should result in a design of the audit methodology to obtain sufficient, appropriate evidence.

   d. Incorrect. Planning the performance audit should be done in a way that assists in identifying and using suitable criteria based on the audit objectives.

2.

    a. Incorrect. Management responsible for corrective action is identified as a primary user of performance audit reports.

    b. Incorrect. Legislators and government officials are identified as primary users of performance audit reports.

    c. Incorrect. The media are identified as primary users of performance audit reports.

    d. Correct. Internal auditors are not specifically identified as primary users of performance audit reports.

3.

    a. Correct. Only controls significant to the audit objectives are required to be assessed.

    b. Incorrect. Obtaining an understanding of significant internal controls is required in the performance audit.

    c. Incorrect. The auditor should assess and document the assessment of the design, implementation, or operating effectiveness of such internal control to the extent necessary to address the audit objectives for significant internal controls.

    d. Incorrect. The auditor should evaluate and document the significance of identified internal control deficiencies within the context of the audit objectives.

Chapter 9

Knowledge check solutions

1.

    a. Incorrect. Communicating the results of audits to those charged with governance, the appropriate officials of the audited entity, and the appropriate oversight officials is a purpose of the report.

    b. Incorrect. Facilitating follow-up to determine whether appropriate corrective actions have been taken is a purpose of the report.

    c. Incorrect. Performance audit reports are permitted to be in the form of written reports, letters, or briefing slides.

    d. Correct. Publishing the report electronically for users of the financial statements is not a requirement.

2.

    a. Incorrect. The nature of any confidential or sensitive information omitted from the report is required.

    b. Correct. A statement whether any fraud was identified is not required to be reported.

    c. Incorrect. The audit results, including findings, are required to be reported.

    d. Incorrect. The objectives, scope, and methodology of the audit are required to be reported.

3.

    a. Correct. Deficiencies in internal control that are significant to the audit objectives should be reported.

    b. Incorrect. Issuing an opinion on internal control is not part of a performance audit.

    c. Incorrect. Internal control components that are significant to the audit objectives are required to be part of the performance audit.

    d. Incorrect. Deficiencies in internal control that warrant the attention of those charged with governance are required to be reported.

The AICPA publishes *CPA Letter Daily*, a free e-newsletter published each weekday. The newsletter, which covers the 10-12 most important stories in business, finance, and accounting, as well as AICPA information, was created to deliver news to CPAs and others who work with the accounting profession. Besides summarizing media articles, commentaries, and research results, the e-newsletter links to television broadcasts and videos and features reader polls. *CPA Letter Daily*'s editors scan hundreds of publications and websites, selecting the most relevant and important news so you don't have to. The newsletter arrives in your inbox early in the morning. To sign up, visit smartbrief.com/CPA.

Do you need high-quality technical assistance? The AICPA Auditing and Accounting Technical Hotline provides non-authoritative guidance on accounting, auditing, attestation, and compilation and review standards. The hotline can be reached at 877.242.7212.

Learn More

Continuing Professional Education

Thank you for selecting the American Institute of Certified Public Accountants as your continuing professional education provider. We have a diverse offering of CPE courses to help you expand your skillset and develop your competencies. Choose from hundreds of different titles spanning the major subject matter areas relevant to CPAs and CGMAs, including:

- Governmental and not-for-profit accounting, auditing, and updates
- Internal control and fraud
- Audits of employee benefit plans and 401(k) plans
- Individual and corporate tax updates
- A vast array of courses in other areas of accounting and auditing, controllership, management, consulting, taxation, and more!

Get your CPE when and where you want

- Self-study training options that includes on-demand, webcasts, and text formats with superior quality and a broad portfolio of topics, including bundled products like –
  - ➢ CPExpress® online learning for immediate access to hundreds of one- to four-credit hour online courses for just-in-time learning at a price that is right
  - ➢ Annual Webcast Pass offering live Q&A with experts and unlimited access to the scheduled lineup, all at an incredible discount.
- Staff training programs for audit, tax and preparation, compilation, and review
- Certificate programs offering comprehensive curriculums developed by practicing experts to build fundamental core competencies in specialized topics
- National conferences presented by recognized experts
- Affordable courses on-site at your organization – visit **aicpalearning.org/on-site** for more information.
- Seminars sponsored by your state society and led by top instructors. For a complete list, visit **aicpalearning.org/publicseminar**.

Take control of your career development

The AICPA's Competency and Learning website at **https://competency.aicpa.org** brings together a variety of learning resources and a self-assessment tool, enabling tracking and reporting of progress toward learning goals.

Visit www.AICPAStore.com to browse our CPE selections.

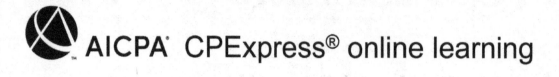

Your strategic learning partner

Let us help prepare your staff for the future.

What is your current approach to learning? One size does not fit all. Your organization is unique, and your approach to learning and competency should be, too. But where do you start? Choose a strategic partner to help you assess competencies and gaps, design a customized learning plan, and measure and maximize the ROI of your learning and development initiatives.

We offer a wide variety of learning programs for finance professionals at every stage of their career.

AICPA Learning resources can help you:

- Create a learning culture to attract and retain talent
- Enrich staff competency and stay current on changing regulations
- Sharpen your competitive edge
- Capitalize on emerging opportunities
- Meet your goals and positively impact your bottom line
- Address CPE/CPD compliance

Flexible learning options include:

- On-site training
- Conferences
- Webcasts
- Certificate programs
- Online self-study
- Publications

An investment in learning can directly impact your bottom line. Contact an AICPA learning consultant to begin your professional development planning.

Call: 800.634.6780, option 1
Email: AICPALearning@aicpa.org